Teachers and
international labour standards:
A handbook

Teachers and international labour standards: A handbook

International Labour Office   Geneva

ILO
Teachers and international labour standards: A handbook
Geneva, International Labour Office, 1990
/Teacher/s, /Working conditions/, /Conditions of employment/, /Teacher status/,
/ILO Convention/s, /ILO Recommendation/s, /Developed country/s, /Developing country/s.
13.11.2
ISBN 92-2-107099-9

ILO Cataloguing in Publication Data

ILO publications can be obtained through major booksellers or ILO local offices in many countries, or direct from ILO Publications, International Labour Office, CH-1211 Geneva 22, Switzerland. A catalogue or list of new publications will be sent free of charge from the above address.

Contents

Introduction

Schools are at the heart of the community, and of nations as a whole, throughout the world. From the infant classes to the end of secondary education, schools are where the adults of tomorrow learn the skills, acquire the knowledge and culture, the will to achieve, that make it possible for societies to advance and at the same time maintain their inherited values.

Organised education in schools needs the respect and support of the community; otherwise it will not fulfil its essential role. To most people the teacher is the symbol of the school. Confidence in the teacher inspires confidence in the quality and utility of the education offered — and vice versa.

The point may seem obvious, but it deserves thought.

Where the status of teachers and the importance of their role is recognised, the morale of the profession is sustained, and this enhances the ability of individual teachers to teach pupils to situate themselves in an increasingly complex world.

Morale slips, on the other hand, in countries where the prestige of the profession has been allowed to decline. This is a risk, for example, wherever the idea takes root that school curricula are not relevant to the needs of society.

When a society puts less value on the education offered, it sets less store by its teachers. One major consequence is that it becomes difficult to recruit good candidates for the profession — and the quality of teaching and of education in general suffers.

Similar problems, common standards

The spread of universal education, and the fact that with the rising demographic curve there are more and more children to be educated — especially in the developing countries — has increased the number of teachers two-and-a-half times in the past 25 years. The profession now numbers close to 40 million men and women world-wide — the population of a medium-sized country.

A diversity of laws, regulations and customs apply to this large profession around the world, yet teachers in all countries have common or similar problems, needs and aspirations.

The need for common standards and measures to govern all aspects of the employment of primary and secondary teachers has long been recognised — by the teaching profession itself, as well as by governments and the international organisations which are directly concerned.

Responsibility for setting these standards and measures and for monitoring their implementation is shared at the international level by the United Nations Educational, Scientific and Cultural Organisation (Unesco) and by the International Labour Organisation (ILO).

Preparation for the teaching profession is a concern of Unesco, while the social and economic situation of teachers falls within the domain of the ILO. Educational policy is in Unesco's sphere of competence, but the employment and terms of service of teachers are matters for the ILO.

The Recommendation concerning the Status of Teachers

The question — tackled jointly by Unesco and the ILO in the 1960s — was how to provide member States of both organisations with an instrument which would deal with all aspects of the employment of teachers, and have the improvement of their status as its aim.

The outcome was the adoption of the *Recommendation concerning the Status of Teachers* at an intergovernmental conference called by Unesco in 1966 and with which the ILO was closely associated. The Recommendation concerns not only the status of teachers; it is about the status and performance of education.

The Recommendation does not impose any obligations on governments; they are invited to draw guidance from it in all matters concerning the teaching profession. In this respect, it resembles the Recommendations adopted by the International Labour Conference and by Unesco, which differ from Conventions in the sense that they do not require ratification by member States.

Member States of both organisations are, however, asked periodically to report on what they have done to bring their education systems into line with the provisions of the Recommendation. The information supplied on such occasions is studied by the Joint ILO/Unesco Committee of Experts on the Application of the Recommendation concerning the Status of Teachers, which has met regularly since 1968.

Positive changes

In the past two decades new teaching methods have been introduced, society itself has changed and, with it, school curricula. The tasks of teachers have also evolved considerably since the 1960s.

The changes have been positive. Governments generally accept that teachers must have a status which corresponds to their key role in the advance of education and to the importance of their contribution to the development of the individual and of society as a whole. Teachers are in many countries better prepared for their careers and have more possibilities of in-service training today than in the 1960s.

Has the Recommendation helped?

How much progress is due to the existence of the 1966 Recommendation? The fact that it seems to be not well enough known is one of the reasons for the publication of this booklet. It may well be that the Joint Committee's insistence on teachers' freedoms — the right to design and update curricula and teaching methods, to participate in the drawing up of educational policy and plans, and particularly the right to freedom of association — has aroused interest in these aspects of the Recommendation. Certainly, the complaints of teachers' organisations to the Committee on Freedom of Association — a supervisory organ of the ILO Governing Body on which governments, employers' and workers' organisations are represented — have become more and more frequent.

There have been calls to strengthen the 1966 Recommendation, to bring it up to date, or to think in terms of a Convention which would have legal force in the countries which ratify it. This is evidence that it has not been ignored.

Without minimising the added strength that a Convention would give, the view of the Joint Committee — shared by the ILO and Unesco and to some extent by teachers' organisations — is that the 1966 Recommendation stands the test of time, and that it continues to have fundamental importance to the teaching profession.

Many of the goals the 1966 Recommendation set were ambitious in the 1960s and are still objectives unrealised over large areas of the world today.

Labour standards and teachers

The fact remains that if educational circles do not know that the 1966 Recommendation exists, or are only vaguely aware of its provisions, the impact it makes on the careers, rewards and working conditions of teachers can only be indirect and minimal.

There are wider implications. All the provisions of the 1966 Recommendation in the ILO's area of competence are based on international labour standards: Conventions and Recommendations adopted by the International Labour Conference since the founding of the ILO in 1919, which apply to teachers as much as to other workers.

International labour standards in several categories have a particular significance for the teaching profession; those, for example, which deal with basic human rights — freedom of association, equal remuneration, and discrimination in respect of employment and occupation — or those concerned with employment policy, vocational guidance and training, and job security.

Given their central role in the shaping of society, teachers — individually and as an occupational group — are also affected by ILO standards dealing with social policy, labour relations, conditions of work and wages, social security, and the employment of women and of older workers.

The purpose of this publication is not only to offer teachers and their organisations — as well as policy-makers, planners and administrators in the field of education — a basic guide to the main provisions of the Recommendation concerning the Status of Teachers, but also more generally to the standards — Conventions and Recommendations — adopted by the International Labour Conference, where they touch on the interests of the teaching profession. The emphasis is on labour standards which have been created since the adoption of the Recommendation in 1966.

It will be noticed that certain standards, proposals or recommendations are relevant to more than one of the major themes covered by the publication. This explains their recurrence in different chapters with, perhaps, a change in the angle of view reflecting a particular significance to the subject under discussion.

Readers who wish to know more about individual ILO Conventions and Recommendations may obtain copies of the texts from the International Labour Office, CH-1211 Geneva 22, Switzerland.

For the sake of clarity, the Recommendation concerning the Status of Teachers is referred to throughout as "the 1966 Recommendation" whereas international standards adopted by the International Labour Conference are described as "Convention No. —" or "Recommendation No. —".

The reference numbers in the text appearing just after the names of particular documents relate to the international labour standards and publications listed in Annex I.

The ABC of labour standards 1

What are international labour standards?

These standards are internationally recognised principles and aims of social policy adopted by the International Labour Conference, which meets annually. There are two types of standard: Conventions and Recommendations. Since the foundation of the ILO in 1919, the Conference (as at 30 June 1990) has adopted 171 Conventions and 178 Recommendations.

What is the difference between a Convention and a Recommendation?

Conventions are open to ratification by governments. Ratification means that a government binds itself to modify national laws to bring them into line with the text of the Convention. Recommendations are intended to guide national policies but lay no formal obligations on governments. Frequently, the Conference adopts a Convention and a Recommendation on the same subject at the same time. Recommendations usually set higher or more detailed standards than Conventions. To be adopted, both Conventions and Recommendations require the approval of two-thirds of the votes at the Conference.

It also happens that only a Recommendation is adopted, in cases where the subject does not lend itself to a Convention, or because the time is not ripe for a Convention. Examples of Recommendations which stand on their own are the Workers' Housing Recommendation, 1961 (No. 115), and the Older Workers Recommendation, 1980 (No. 162).

How is it possible to know that a Convention or Recommendation has been adopted by the International Labour Conference?

Governments are bound to submit both Conventions and Recommendations to the national law-making body — usually parliament — within 12 to 18 months after they have been adopted by the Conference.

Are the interested parties properly represented at the International labour Conference?

Yes. The ILO is unique among United Nations organisations in having a tripartite structure. Each national delegation to the Conference comprises two representatives of the government, and one each from the most representative employers' and workers' organisations. In addition, the drafting of a new Convention or Recommendation calls for the participation of all three groups — separately or collectively — at every stage.

What has been the impact of international labour standards on national legislation?

There is no country where social policies do not bear the imprint of at least some ILO standards. The first point to note is that there had been 5,463 ratifications of ILO Conventions by the end of 1989. This means that, in principle, the standards required by the Conventions in each case had been incorporated in national laws — or that the government firmly intends to bring legislation into line with the labour standard.

Secondly, it has been shown that the existence of an ILO Convention — ratified or not — or of a Recommendation creates a yardstick for national measures. This may even be true when standards are only at the stage of discussion.

How is it possible to know that the standards really are applied?

The ILO checks on the performance of governments in applying standards. Under the ILO Constitution, member States have the obligation to report on the action they have taken to put into effect the Conventions they ratify, and the national workers' and employers' organisations, which receive copies of the official reports, may in turn make their own comments.

The ILO also calls on governments to report on the effect they are giving to unratified Conventions as well as Recommendations. Hundreds of changes in laws and practices have been made as a result of the annual review of the application of Conventions carried out by an independent panel of international jurists and by a standing committee of the International Labour Conference.

Many other changes have been made after the investigation by the ILO of complaints by national or international employers' or workers' organisations of violations of ratified Conventions.

In addition, the ILO offers expert advice to governments which ask for help in overcoming problems they encounter in putting Conventions into practice.

Finally, the ILO can call on governments to report on the effect they are giving to unratified Conventions and to Recommendations.

Is there a way of making sure that, at the national level, governments consult employers' and workers' organisations on matters connected with ILO standards?

There is. The Tripartite Consultation (International Labour Standards) Convention, 1976 (No. 144) and its accompanying Recommendation (No. 152),[28] provide that there shall be consultations with the workers and employers on government proposals concerning the agenda of the International Labour Conference and on all points which arise over the making of Conventions and Recommendations, their implementation, the reports that have to be submitted to the ILO and the possible denunciation of a ratified Convention.

Are ILO standards revised to keep up with changing social and economic circumstances?

Yes. Standards are constantly being reviewed, and whenever necessary, the Conference is asked to adopt new or revised Conventions or Recommendations which should not merely reflect the current situation, but which look to the future.

Has the character of ILO standards changed over the past 70 years?

In one important sense, yes. For the first few years, the ILO's legislation was designed to protect the worker against exploitation and harsh, unjust working conditions. The early Conventions dealt, typically, with subjects such as hours of work, night work, protection against industrial accidents, and the elimination of child labour and forced labour.

Increasingly, ILO standards have turned to the promotion of basic human rights and policies for social advancement. There are, for example, Conventions covering freedom of association, the right to organise and bargain collectively, freedom from discrimination, employment policy, equal pay for work of equal value, minimum standards of social security and labour-management relations, while, at the same time, other Conventions fulfil the need for new standards in traditional areas as the world undergoes new technological and social changes.

Employment and career

2

As a central issue for the teaching profession, employment and career prospects feature prominently in the 1966 ILO/Unesco Recommendation, [1] which takes as its starting-point two basic assumptions:
— education is a service of fundamental importance in the general public interest and an essential factor in economic growth; and
— education must feature in overall economic and social planning and receive an adequate share of national income.

The 1966 Recommendation does not stand alone. The principles it sets forth are based on international labour standards — ILO Conventions and Recommendations — which have as direct a bearing on the employment and careers of teachers as of other workers.

Facing up to the issues

In recent years the ILO has addressed the concerns of teachers through studies and consultations dealing specifically with their situation. Some of its general surveys — on equity in employment and occupation, [56] for example — are also highly relevant.

The ILO Joint Meeting on Conditions of Work of Teachers, held in Geneva in 1981, [45] related general standards to specific conditions in the teaching profession. It reviewed many of the subjects which are covered in this chapter, and it also took up the questions of employment trends in the profession, teacher surpluses, unemployment and shortages.

The meeting considered that no effort should be spared to ensure that suitably qualified teachers are available in numbers which measure up to the size and educational needs of the school population. It also put emphasis on security and stability of employment, as an indispensable means of attracting and keeping good teachers, and of maintaining and improving professional standards.

A better statistical base was needed, the participants agreed, to permit proper forecasting of staff needs and to avoid mismatches between teachers and teaching jobs.

Staff surpluses ...

In its conclusions, the meeting stated that reductions in education budgets and redundancies should be avoided wherever possible. Preferably, when there is a surplus of teachers, the intake into the profession and into teacher training should be reduced — although such measures should be kept to a minimum and ended or eased as soon as possible. Other steps which might be taken to deal with surpluses include:

— paid educational leave for teachers;
— shortening of teaching hours for new entrants (and also, if they so wished, for teachers approaching retirement);
— reduction in the size of classes, pupil-teacher ratios or both;
— creation of new types of posts within the profession;
— making it possible for full-time teachers to work part time temporarily; and
— transfers to other schools or to other work within the education system.

If redundancies become unavoidable, certain steps should be taken. These include consultations with teachers' organisations, the provision of financial indemnities and retraining, and giving preferential treatment to teachers made redundant when filling new vacancies.

The meeting noted the vulnerability of teachers in private schools and new entrants everywhere. To protect new entrants, fixed-term, temporary and part-time appointments should be kept to a minimum.

In practice, however, a number of factors, including budget cuts and structural adjustments, have produced a situation in which there are growing numbers of teachers without established posts or serving on a part-time basis. Women teachers, who constitute an important part of the profession, are particularly affected.

... and shortages

Shortages of teachers tend to occur in developing countries which are introducing universal education and which have an expanding school population. They also arise, however, in specific subject areas in both developed and developing countries, and in situations where economic slow-downs or lack of job opportunities encourage pupils to extend their education rather than face the prospect of unemployment.

To counter shortages, the 1981 meeting proposed in its conclusions that:

— conditions of work and employment for teachers should stand comparison with those in other occupations in order to attract persons with the necessary abilities and to keep them in the profession;

— salaries, pensions and other social security benefits are powerful incentives;

— recruitment of inadequately qualified teachers should be avoided in both continuing and temporary situations of shortage; and

— reasonable class sizes and hours of teaching should be established to avoid aggravating shortages by harming the performance and health of the staff and causing dissatisfaction.

Teachers as public servants

A large majority of teachers are public employees, and are governed either by civil service law or by ordinary labour law. Their concerns are reflected, with those of other civil servants, in the debates and conclusions of the ILO's Joint Committee on the Public Service, which held its Fourth Session in Geneva in 1988. [54]

The Committee deals thoroughly in its reports with questions such as disciplinary codes and procedures; recruitment, training and career development; the situation of women in public service; and the effects of structural and technological progress on government employment.

Among other conclusions, the Committee states that temporary staff should only be employed in exceptional circumstances, and that non-established (tenured) workers who are permanently employed should be considered for early establishment (tenure), with length of previous service taken into account. Part-time work should not be seen as a means of exploiting cheap labour.

In recruitment, there should be no discrimination of any kind, and equality of opportunity for men and women should be promoted in all aspects of employment, access to training and promotion.

Noting that women form a substantial part of the labour force in public services and that they tend to predominate among temporary, non-established and part-time staff, the Committee has called for the elimination of all forms of discrimination based on sex; equal pay for equal work; equal opportunities for women to be employed in all sectors and in all kinds of jobs; and that, for both men and women, measures be taken to reconcile the demands of family and working life.

International standards

The Conventions and Recommendations adopted by the International Labour Conference are an indispensable guide for action on employment and career prospects at the national level for all working people. Some of these international labour standards are fundamental in character, dealing, for example, with the issues of employment policy and discrimination. Others have a more specific application. In each case, they have something important to say to the teaching profession.

The essential characteristics of a number of Conventions and Recommendations which cover the issues of employment and career prospects, and the corresponding provisions of the 1966 Recommendation concerning the Status of Teachers are described below.

Employment policy

The basic ILO standards on employment policy for all categories of workers, including teachers, were established in the Employment Policy Convention, 1964 (No. 122), in its accompanying Recommendation (No. 122) and in the Employment Policy (Supplementary Provisions) Recommendation, 1984 (No. 169). [16]

A policy to promote full, productive and freely chosen employment as the realisation of the right to work becomes a major goal for States which ratify the Convention. Each worker must have the fullest possible opportunity to qualify for, and use his or her skills and endowments in, a job for which he or she is well suited, and without discrimination.

Consultation with representatives of the persons affected by action taken under the policy — particularly representatives of employers and workers — is a feature of the Convention.

The general measures proposed in Recommendation No. 122 to promote employment have as their aim the continued expansion and stability of national economies, coupled in the short term with action to counteract flagging economic activity and inflationary pressures.

Selectively, steps should be taken to even out seasonal fluctuations in employment and the growth of unemployment or underemployment as a result of structural change. Special attention should be given to youth unemployment, and to the employment problems of older or disabled workers, or those who find it difficult to change residence or occupation.

The employment and income needs of depressed areas where large numbers of workers are affected by structural change also call for attention, so as to bring about a better balance of economic activity.

Technological progress and improved productivity lead to greater possibilities of leisure and education. The Recommendation suggests that to take advantage of these developments, consideration should be given to reducing hours of work without a decrease in wages, to longer paid holidays, and later entry into the labour force, combined with more advanced education and training.

In developing countries, the Recommendation states, employment policy should be an essential element of a policy to promote growth and the fair sharing of national incomes. It makes specific proposals on investment and income policies, and the promotion of industrial and rural employment in these countries. It also invokes the problem of rapid population growth, and the need for international action to promote employment objectives.

Population policy was a major theme, 20 years later, in Recommendation No. 169. [16] It proposes that attention should be given, particularly in developing countries, to the education of actual and potential parents on the benefits of family planning. In rural areas family planning services with trained staff should be increased. In urban areas the urgent need for appropriate infrastructures and improved living conditions in slums should receive special attention.

Measures are suggested to improve employment opportunities for women, young workers, the disabled, older workers, the long-term unemployed and migrants. These include the creation of vocational guidance and training programmes which link the educational system with the world of work, programmes to create gainful employment in specific sectors, and the promotion of self-employment and workers' co-operatives.

For young people, action might include voluntary work on community projects, and programmes offering an alternation of training and work to make it easier to find the first job.

National development policies should favour the introduction of appropriate technologies, and there should be employment promotion programmes to encourage family work and independent work, in recognition of the importance of the informal sector as a provider of jobs. Likewise, the contribution of small enterprises and of local employment-creation initiatives to the fight against unemployment should be recognised.

Recommendation No. 169 also argues for balanced growth through regional development policies, and for the utility of public investment and special public works programmes as a means of maintaining employment, raising incomes, reducing poverty and meeting basic needs.

Among international measures, it suggests aims for ILO member States in promoting the expansion of world trade as a means of helping one another to maintain the growth of employment.

On international migration, Recommendation No. 169 proposes that more employment and better conditions of work be created in countries of emigration to reduce the need to seek work elsewhere. Migration should take place under conditions which promote full, productive and freely chosen employment. Countries which habitually admit foreign workers should help the "supply" countries to develop in ways that will produce alternatives to migration.

Other international labour standards which are designed to help ILO member States to implement their employment policies include: the Employment Service Convention, 1948 (No. 88), and its accompanying Recommendation (No. 83), [4] and the Labour Administration Convention, 1978 (No. 150), and its accompanying Recommendation (No. 158), [30] which deal with the setting up and operation of employment services and the organisation of labour administration.

Equality of opportunity and non-discrimination

All aspects of the preparation and employment of teachers should be free from any form of discrimination on the grounds of race, colour, sex, religion, political opinion, national or social origin or economic condition, in the words of the 1966 Recommendation.

This principle was established over 30 years ago in the Discrimination (Employment and Occupation) Convention, 1958 (No. 111) — which has been ratified by 111 countries — and in its accompanying Recommendation (No. 111). [10] These are basic human rights instruments which promote equality of opportunity and treatment by seeking to eliminate all forms of discrimination in employment. The Convention's protection extends to access to vocational training, access to employment and to particular occupations — and it covers all individuals, without exception. In the Convention, distinction, exclusion or preference based on the inherent requirements of a particular job is not regarded as discrimination.

On ratification, a State undertakes to:

— repeal laws and modify instructions and practices which are not in line with the Convention;

— bring in legislation which will give effect to the Convention;

— engage in educational work to popularise the new policy and, in so doing, seek the co-operation of employers' and workers' organisations; and

— set the policy in employment, vocational guidance, vocational training and placement under the control of national authorities.

The situation of equality in employment and occupation was comprehensively surveyed by the ILO in 1988. A report to the International Labour Conference [56] reviews the application of Convention No. 111 and Recommendation No. 111, gives detailed information on national laws and practices, and draws attention to the problems still to be overcome.

Appointment of teachers

States are offered a set of criteria on the appointment of teachers in the 1966 Recommendation:

— educational policy should be based on the need to provide society with an adequate number of teachers;

— school authorities, in co-operation with teacher-preparation institutions, should see that newly trained teachers are provided with employment in keeping with their preparation, individual wishes and circumstances;

— the normal duration of a probationary period should be known to the probationer in advance; satisfactory completion of probation should be related strictly to professional competence; and

— a teacher who fails to complete probation satisfactorily should be informed of the reasons, and have the right to make representations.

Promotion and assessment

The standpoint taken in the 1966 Recommendation is clear-cut: promotion should be based on an objective assessment of a teacher's qualifications for a new post, by reference to strictly professional criteria laid down in consultation with teachers' organisations.

Other factors which are less easy to assess — character, personality, attitude — are often taken into account, and the Joint ILO/Unesco Committee on the Application of the Recommendation believes that they should be defined as clearly as possible.

When direct assessment of a teacher's work is needed, the 1966 Recommendation states, it must be objective and be made known to the teacher. There should be a right of appeal by teachers against assessments they consider to be unjustified.

The issue of promotion arises in a more general sense, applying to all workers including teachers, in the Human Resources Development Recommendation, 1975 (No. 150). [27] This specifies that in meeting the needs of everyone for vocational training throughout life, States should give particular attention to opportunities for promotion. Further training should enable individuals to improve their performance or broaden their capacities, update their knowledge and skills, in order to move on to higher-level work or gain promotion.

There is a specific reference to further education for teachers in the 1966 Recommendation. Courses and facilities should be designed to enable teachers to improve their qualifications and to seek promotion.

Vocational guidance and vocational training

Vocational training for teachers is, at the international level, a Unesco responsibility. The Human Resources Development Convention, 1975 (No. 142), and its accompanying Recommendation No. 150, [27] however, call for comprehensive and co-ordinated policies and programmes of vocational guidance and vocational training which affect teachers in their own careers as much as other workers, as well as in their capacity as educators of others.

Recommendation No. 150 sets out the aims of these policies and programmes. It states that workers being trained should receive adequate allowances and be covered by social security. (If they are being trained off the job, educational leave should be granted under the terms of the Paid Educational Leave Convention, 1974 (No. 140), and its accompanying Recommendation No. 148.[26])

Vocational guidance and training must be free of discrimination. This principle in Convention No. 142 is spelled out in Recommendation No. 150, which offers measures to promote equality of opportunity for women and migrant workers in training — and through training, in employment.

Dealing with opportunities for women, Recommendation No. 150 speaks of the need to change traditional attitudes to the roles of the sexes in the home and in working life. The whole range of educational, vocational training and employment opportunities should be open to girls and women. They should have equal access to education and training, including preparation for occupations that have traditionally been accessible only to boys and men.

Day-care and other services should be available for children, and vocational training should be provided for women above the normal age of entry into employment who want to go out to work for the first time or return after a period of absence. This provision is made all the more important by the high proportion of women in the teaching profession.

The training of staff for vocational guidance and vocational training activities are also covered in Recommendation No. 150.

Security of employment

In the interests of education and of the teachers, stability of employment and security of tenure are essential, the 1966 Recommendation states. Teachers should be protected against arbitrary action affecting their professional standing or career.

In the Termination of Employment Convention, 1982 (No. 158),[36] the employment of a worker may not be terminated unless there is a valid reason connected with the capacity or conduct of the workers or based on the operational requirements of the enterprise or service.

Although the Convention applies to all employed persons, there are possible exceptions. These include fixed-term contracts and those for specified tasks, probationary periods and casual labour — exemptions which may affect teachers.

However, a possible loophole is closed; there is a clause which states that there must be safeguards against the use of contracts for a specified period of time if the aim is to circumvent the Convention.

Employment should not be terminated on the grounds of:
— membership of a union;
— taking part in union activities outside working hours (or within working hours if the employer has given consent);
— seeking office, or acting, as a workers' representative;
— filing a complaint or taking part in proceedings against an employer;
— race, colour, sex, marital status, family responsibilities, pregnancy, religion, political opinion, national extraction or social origin;
— absence from work during maternity leave; or
— temporary absence because of illness or injury.

Procedures to be followed before, and at the time of, termination are outlined in the Convention, which also provides for the hearing of appeals against termination by an impartial body.

Appeals

A worker who appeals should not have to bear the burden of proof alone. If the termination is found to be unjustified and cannot be reversed, or if reinstatement is not practicable, compensation should be paid.

A reasonable period of notice or equivalent compensation should be allowed when a worker's services are to be terminated and, on leaving, he or she should receive a severance allowance or social security benefit in line with national law and practice.

The Convention also deals with the termination of employment for economic, technological, structural and similar reasons. Here, the employer is required to inform the workers' representatives of the situation in good time and to consult them on ways of avoiding terminations or of cushioning the blow. It is also the employer's duty to inform the competent authority as early as possible if terminations are likely to take place — a point which may concern private educational establishments in particular.

Recommendation No. 166,[36] which accompanies Convention No. 158, states that an employer should consult the workers' representatives when planning major changes in the enterprise which may lead to numerous terminations. It also proposes steps which may avoid or lessen the effect of terminations. These are to restrict hiring, spread the staff cuts over a period, make internal transfers, train and retrain workers, offer voluntary early retirement with income protection, restrict overtime, and reduce normal hours of work.

Apart from the question of termination, the 1966 Recommendation establishes the teacher's right to appeal against disciplinary measures, and lays down standards and safeguards for the procedures to be followed.

Family responsibilities

The difficulties of combining a job with family responsibilities are a major obstacle in the way of achieving equal opportunities for men and women. Measures to do away with discrimination in training and access to employment, as well as in working conditions, often produce only limited results if workers have to give up their jobs or forgo advancement on account of family commitments.

All too often, interruptions in a teaching career for family reasons lead to a loss of seniority and reduced chances of promotion.

The 1966 Recommendation lays stress on the job security and opportunities of women teachers:

— marriage should not be considered a bar to appointment or continued employment, nor should it affect remuneration or other conditions of work;

— contracts should not be terminated on account of pregnancy and maternity leave;

— nursery or crèche arrangements should be considered;

— women with family responsibilities should be given appointments near their homes, and married couples, both teaching, should be assigned to the same neighbourhood or school; and

— women with family responsibilities who have left the profession before retirement age should be encouraged to return.

Equality of the sexes

The distinction between men and women workers with family responsibilities is disappearing, and there have been suggestions in recent years that the 1966 Recommendation be reworded in this sense.

However, men and women are put on an equal footing in the Workers with Family Responsibilities Convention, 1981 (No. 156), and Recommendation No. 165 which accompanies it.[35]

These two instruments form part of a series adopted by the ILO in recent years to promote equality of treatment and opportunity for categories of workers who suffer from particular disadvantages.

"Family responsibilities" are defined as commitments to dependent children or, if they need care and support, other members of the immediate family, where the worker's capacity to prepare for, enter, participate or advance in some economic activity is restricted.

It becomes an aim of national policy for States which ratify the Convention to make it possible for people who want to be employed — or who are working — to exercise their right to do so without discrimination, and without conflict between their jobs and family responsibilities.

As far as possible, workers with family responsibilities should have the same right as others to a free choice of employment, and the chance to stay at work — or to be reintegrated after an absence imposed by family obligations.

The Convention speaks of the need to think of the terms and conditions of employment and social security for such workers, and also of community services, including child care.

Recommendation No. 165 goes several steps further. It proposes education to encourage the sharing of family responsibilities between men and women, and measures which make it easier to reconcile work with family life. These include the progressive reduction of working hours and more flexible work schedules, rest periods and holidays.

When workers are being transferred from one locality to another, factors which should be taken into account include the place of work of the spouse and children's education. Family commitments should be considered when deciding whether an unemployment benefit is to be lost or suspended on the grounds that the worker has refused a suitable offer of employment.

Either parent, according to Recommendation No. 165, should have the possibility to obtain leave of absence immediately after maternity leave. Either parent should be able to obtain leave of absence when a dependent child is sick.

Recommendation No. 165 broke new ground for the ILO in dealing, for the first time in an international labour standard, with the conditions of part-time and temporary workers, many of whom have family responsibilities. They should enjoy the same terms and conditions as those of full-time and permanent workers — calculated on a pro rata basis where appropriate, according to the Recommendation. Part-time workers should be given the option of full-time employment when there is a vacancy and if the circumstances requiring part-time work no longer exist.

In the 1966 Recommendation it is stated that part-time service should be used only if needed, and provided by qualified teachers who for some reason cannot give full-time service. Regular part-timers should receive proportionately the same remuneration and enjoy the same conditions of employment as full-time teachers. They should have paid holidays, sick and maternity leave, and social security protection, which would include pension coverage.

Older workers

The situation of workers who meet difficulties in their employment because of advancing age should, in the ILO's view, be handled as part of a national employment policy and, at the level of the enterprise as a matter of social policy, to avoid merely shifting the problem from one group of workers to another.

The Older Workers Recommendation, 1982 (No. 162),[32] lays down that they should enjoy equality of opportunity and treatment. There should be no discrimination against them in employment and occupation, but special protection or assistance recognised as necessary for older workers should not be affected.

Among the fields specified for equality of treatment with others are training, promotion, job security, remuneration, social security and social services. Older workers should also have equality in access to employment in both the public and private sectors — although age limits may be set in exceptional cases because of the special requirements, conditions or rules of certain types of employment.

Disabled persons

The ILO has been active for a long time in rehabilitation of the disabled, both from the point of view of labour legislation and in providing advisory and technical co-operation services to governments in many parts of the world.

The Vocational Rehabilitation (Disabled) Recommendation, 1955 (No. 99), and the Vocational Rehabilitation and Employment (Disabled Persons) Convention, 1983 (No. 159), and the accompanying Recommendation No. 168[37] are comprehensive, and some of their provisions are of direct concern to the teaching profession.

The purpose of vocational rehabilitation, for States which ratify the Convention, is to enable a disabled person to secure, retain and advance in employment, with social integration as the aim.

A national policy covering all categories of the disabled is required. This policy will promote employment opportunities for the disabled, respect the principle of equal opportunity between the disabled and non-disabled, and between men and women with disabilities. The policy should be put into effect in consultation with organisations of workers, employers and disabled persons.

The Convention also requires the national authorities to provide vocational guidance, vocational training, placement, and employment services which will make it possible for the disabled to find and retain jobs as well as to move forward in their careers. Existing services — adapted as necessary — are to be used wherever possible.

The Recommendations are more detailed. Recommendation No. 168 emphasises the need to start early with vocational rehabilitation. To make this possible, health care and other bodies responsible for medical and social rehabilitation should co-operate with those responsible for vocational rehabilitation.

Physical and other kinds of barriers and obstacles should be eliminated if they make it difficult for disabled people to move about, be trained, or take jobs, and there should be standards which take this need into account in the design of new buildings and facilities. This provision finds an echo in the 1966 Recommendation which states that school buildings should be safe and attractive in overall design and functional in layout.

The Recommendation's provisions on the status of staff engaged in vocational rehabilitation and the training of disabled persons are of particular interest to the teaching profession. Their training, qualifications and remuneration should be comparable to those of teachers engaged in general vocational training with similar duties and responsibilities.

Career opportunities should also be comparable and the transfer of staff between vocational rehabilitation and general vocational training should be encouraged.

Wherever fully trained staff are not available in sufficient numbers, aides and auxiliaries may be recruited and trained. They should not, however, be a permanent substitute for fully trained staff. They should, as far as possible, be given further training and integrated into the qualified staff.

Labour relations 3

Although the right of teachers to organise, to negotiate or to be consulted is still not universally accepted, it is not difficult to find international legal instruments, recommendations and decisions which confirm that in this respect they do not differ in any way from other workers.

The right to organise

> Workers and employers, without distinction whatsoever, shall have the right to establish and, subject only to the rules of the organisation concerned, to join organisations of their own choosing without previous authorisation.

The above wording, from the widely ratified Freedom of Association and Protection of the Right to Organise Convention, 1948 (No. 87), [3] could hardly be more explicit.

Workers' and employers' organisations, according to the Convention, must have the right to draw up their own constitutions and rules, to elect their representatives in full freedom, to organise their administration and activities and formulate their programmes without interference by the public authorities. They may not be dissolved or suspended by administrative authority, and they have the right to form federations and confederations, and to affiliate with international organisations.

A year later the ILO adopted a second Convention dealing with the basic human right of freedom of association: the Right to Organise and Collective Bargaining Convention, 1949 (No. 98), [6] which states that workers shall be protected against acts of anti-union discrimination. It forbids interference by workers' or employers' organisations in each other's establishment, functioning or administration. Workers' organisations shall also be protected against interference of a kind which will place them under the domination of employers. This Convention has been ratified by a substantial majority of ILO member States.

Where is it stated that these international labour standards apply to teachers — in public as well as in private employment? The 1966

Recommendation[1] says so quite clearly — and takes the matter further. A major point made by the Recommendation is that teachers' organisations should be recognised as a force which can contribute greatly to advances in education.

In a further step, the ILO's Freedom of Association Committee[51] has confirmed that the administrative staff of national education services as well as teachers should be protected by Convention No. 98.

However, the Joint ILO/Unesco Committee of Experts on the Application of the Recommendation concerning the Status of Teachers notes that, in several countries, teachers in public schools (i.e. State schools) do not yet have the right to organise.

Workers' representatives

Since 1966, other instruments have been adopted by the ILO which reinforce the right to organise of teachers — as of other workers. The Workers' Representatives Convention, 1971 (No. 135), and its accompanying Recommendation No. 143[23] provide that trade union delegates or other freely elected representatives of the workers of an enterprise shall be protected against victimisation in the form of acts prejudicial to them, including dismissal, based on their status or activities and that they shall have the facilities they need to carry out their functions.

Where both trade union and non-union elected representatives are present in the same enterprise, Recommendation No. 143 states that co-operation between the two types of representative should be encouraged, and that steps should be taken to avoid undermining the position of the unions.

While these ILO standards do not refer specifically to teachers, it can be assumed that they apply to schools, both public and private. The ILO's Committee of Experts on the Application of Conventions and Recommendations has observed (in a case concerning the application of Convention No. 135 to a charitable health institution managed by a church) that the Convention "presupposes that no obstacle can be placed in the way of the appointment of workers' representatives in an undertaking (whatever its status)".[44]

The Committee has asked States that have ratified the Convention to provide information on its application to public servants and employees in public corporations,[46] among whom are found the majority of teachers.

Union activity: A civic right

The liberty of teachers to participate in social and public life is taken in the 1966 Recommendation to include the professional organisations which represent their interests.

In the wider sense, society and the education service benefit when teachers take part in community activities; the personal development of individual teachers is also enhanced.

Teachers have the same civic rights as all other citizens and should not be penalised for exercising them. When a teacher has to give up his or her normal work on election or appointment to public office, the 1966 Recommendation states, he or she should be retained in the profession for seniority and pension purposes. In such cases the teacher should be able to take up his or her previous post or its equivalent on the expiry of the term of public office.

Where bodies representing the teaching profession are concerned, the 1966 Recommendation states that teachers should:

— be granted occasional leave of absence with full pay to enable them to participate in the activities of their organisations; and

— have the right to take up office in these organisations.

Education ministry staff

Convention No. 98 fully covers the right to organise of teachers and the administrative staff of schools. Another ILO instrument, the Labour Relations (Public Service) Convention, 1978 (No. 151), [31] is of interest to civil servants in government ministries, including those responsible for education, because it applies to nearly all persons employed by the authorities in a category that Convention No. 98 excludes: public servants engaged in the administration of the State.

Convention No. 151 covers all persons employed by public authorities, although national legislation may exclude — along with the armed forces and police — high-level employees with policy-making or managerial functions and those with highly confidential duties. It protects the right of public employees to organise by stating that they shall not suffer from anti-union discrimination, particularly through acts which make employment conditional on not joining or giving up membership of a public employees' organisation, or which lead to dismissal because of union membership or activities.

Organisations of public employees shall enjoy independence of the authorities, the Convention states, and be protected against interference, particularly of a kind which seeks to put them under official domination. Representatives of recognised organisations of public employees shall be provided with facilities to carry out their functions, within and outside working hours, in such a way that the efficient operation of the administration or service concerned is not affected.

Negotiation

To establish, once and for all, the right to organise is one purpose of Convention No. 98. Its second aim is to confirm the right to collective bargaining between social partners.

So that the terms and conditions of employment may be regulated by collective agreements, the Convention calls for measures to encourage and promote the development and use of machinery for voluntary negotiation between employers or their organisations on the one hand and workers' organisations on the other.

In its most recent survey of the application of ILO Conventions on freedom of association,[46] the ILO Committee of Experts on the Application of Conventions and Recommendations has stressed that trade unions must have the right to negotiate wages and conditions of employment freely with employers and their organisations.

Government interference with the process nevertheless is not unknown, and it increasingly takes the form of restrictions on the scope of bargaining or of making it necessary to have official approval to apply agreements that have been negotiated. These practices, in the view of the Committee of Experts on the Application of Conventions and Recommendations, are contrary to the provisions of Convention No. 98, and to the general principle that organisations have the right to develop their own activities and formulate their programmes.

Relevance to teachers

The 1966 Recommendation related the right to bargain collectively in Convention No. 98 to the situation of teachers. The Recommendation states that salaries and working conditions for teachers should be negotiated between teachers' organisations and both public and private employers, and that this right should be assured by the establishment of statutory or voluntary machinery.

The Recommendation proposes that no merit-rating system for use in determining salaries should be introduced or applied without consultation beforehand and the agreement of the teachers' organisations concerned.

Not all governments, however, share these views. In several countries teachers in public schools do not have the right to negotiate their employment and working conditions.

Teachers' workload

Teachers in many countries are consulted by their employers, in one way or another, on the fixing of their hours of work. The authorities in other countries do not deal with teachers' organisations on this important aspect of working conditions — although the 1966 Recommendation suggests they should do so. The Joint ILO/Unesco Committee of Experts on the Application of the Recommendation[55] has stated that the workload of teachers should be settled by negotiation.

Although generally recognised in the private sector, the right to negotiate salaries and conditions is not always conceded to public servants and their organisations. For this reason, ILO Convention No. 151 states that:

> measures ... shall be taken ... to encourage and promote the full development and utilisation of machinery for negotiation of terms and conditions of employment between the public authorities concerned and public employees'organisations, or of such other methods as will allow representatives of public employees to participate in the determination of these matters.

This way of expressing a commitment to collective bargaining is less forthright than the wording of Convention No. 98. The important point to note, however, is that Convention No. 151 is only to be applied to the extent that more favourable provisions in other international Conventions are not applicable.

The Committee of Experts on the Application of Conventions and Recommendations has decided in a case concerning the setting of teachers' pay and conditions that if a country has ratified both Conventions, the more favourable provision in Convention No. 98 should be preferred.[56]

Promotion of collective bargaining

In a further move to strengthen the means of negotiation between workers and employers in all branches of economic activity, the ILO adopted the Collective Bargaining Convention, 1981 (No. 154).[33]

This Convention covers all negotiations between an employer, group of employers or employers' organisations on the one hand and one or more workers' organisations to:

— determine working conditions and terms of employment;
— regulate relations between employers and workers; and
— regulate relations between employers or their organisations and organisation(s) of workers.

Only the armed forces and the police may be excluded from the scope of the Convention in the countries which ratify it. "Special modalities of application" for the public service may be fixed by national laws, regulations or practice.

The central feature of Convention No. 154 is that measures should be taken to promote collective bargaining. The aims should be to:

— open the possibility of collective bargaining to all employers and groups of workers;

— encourage the establishing of rules of procedure agreed between employers' and workers' organisations; and

— design bodies and procedures for the settlement of labour disputes so as to contribute to the promotion of collective bargaining.

In applying the Convention, the public authorities should consult employers' and workers' organisations in advance, and try to come to all-round agreement with them. The principle that public and private employers and the public authorities should disclose the information needed to make negotiations meaningful is brought out in the Collective Bargaining Recommendation, 1981 (No. 163), [33] which supplements Convention No. 154. This Recommendation also underlines the need for the parties involved in collective bargaining to provide their representatives with the necessary mandate to conduct and conclude negotiations.

Complaints procedures and ILO standards

The ILO has established special procedures to examine complaints by employers' or workers' organisations that they are not able to exercise properly their right to organise and bargain collectively.

Generally speaking, a complaint against a State cannot be received by the ILO unless the country concerned has ratified the appropriate ILO Convention. To respond to trade union demands that something be done to overcome this problem, the Fact-Finding and Conciliation Commission on Freedom of Association was established in 1950. However, the Commission has met rarely because it cannot operate, in the absence of a ratification, without the consent of the State concerned.

The Committee on Freedom of Association of the ILO's Governing Body, on the other hand, deals with complaints whether or not a Convention has been ratified by the State concerned, and the State's consent is not required for the matter to be considered.

Complaints, backed by evidence, must come from national workers' or employers' organisations, or from an international workers' or employers' body which has consultative status with the ILO, for example the International Confederation of Free Trade Unions (ICFTU), the World Confederation of Labour (WCL), the World Federation of Trade Unions (WFTU), or the Organisation of African Trade Union Unity (OATUU). However, international organisations without consultative status, including the international teachers' organisations — the World Federation of Teachers' Unions (FISE), the International Federation of Free Teachers' Unions (IFFTU), the World Confederation of Organisations of the Teaching Profession (WCOTP) and the World Confederation of Teachers (WCT) — may also lodge complaints with the Committee if the allegations concern matters directly affecting one of their affiliates. The Committee presents its conclusions and recommendations for the settlement of complaints to the ILO Governing Body.

The work of the Committee, which consists of three members chosen for their personal attributes by each of the groups represented in the ILO's tripartite structure — workers, employers and governments — has grown over the years. There is now a substantial body of decisions by the Committee on the application of the freedom of association Conventions. These interpretations are all the more important to teachers because a sizeable number of the complaints in recent years have been lodged by national or international teachers' organisations. **In a series of cases, the Committee has upheld the right of teachers, including school administrative staff, to engage in collective bargaining.**

On the other hand, the Committee has pointed out that determining the broad lines of educational policy does not come within the scope of collective bargaining, although it would be normal to consult teachers' organisations on these matters.

Consultation

International labour standards repeatedly return to the theme of consultation as a means of preserving labour peace and ensuring that social justice becomes a reality. This is a concern for the public authorities as much as for employers' and workers' organisations.

One set of guide-lines which can be directly applied to the situation of the teaching profession is in the Consultation (Industrial and National Levels)

Recommendation, 1960 (No. 113). [11] The Recommendation says that the public authorities should seek the views, advice and assistance of employers' and workers' organisations in:
— the preparation and implementation of laws and regulations affecting their interests;
— the establishment and functioning of national bodies, including those which organise employment, vocational training and retraining, labour protection, health and safety, productivity, social security and welfare; and
— the drawing up and execution of plans for economic and social development.

The conference which adopted the Recommendation concerning the Status of Teachers in 1966 saw consultation in various forms as a means of improving the quality of education.

The 1966 Recommendation, for example, calls on teachers and teachers' organisations to co-operate with the authorities in the interests of the pupils, of the education service and of society generally.

In more specific terms, the 1966 Recommendation suggests that teachers' organisations should help to establish standards of performance for the profession: a code of ethics similar to those which exist for magistrates, lawyers and doctors.

It also proposes that the authorities consult regularly with representative teachers' bodies on educational policy and objectives, school organisation and new developments in the education service. The areas covered would include educational research and the introduction of new methods, the development of new courses, the choice of textbooks and teaching aids.

Teachers, the 1966 Recommendation says, should be encouraged to work together in panels within schools or over wider areas, and the authorities should listen to their opinions and suggestions on specific educational questions.

The 1966 Recommendation also suggests efforts to establish good relations and mutual understanding between the administrative staff of education services and teachers.

In-service education

Teachers' organisations should be consulted by the authorities when they set up further education activities for the profession. In-service education for teachers is a key aspect of the 1966 Recommendation. It should be free and available to all, and bodies representing the profession should have a hand in the way it is run. Refresher courses should be provided, especially for teachers returning to class work after a break in service.

Recruitment policy is another area in which the 1966 Recommendation proposes co-operation between teachers' organisations and the authorities — although this does not yet occur in more than a few countries — as well as the setting of professional criteria for promotion.

Teachers' organisations should also be consulted, the 1966 Recommendation proposes, when the authorities set up official machinery to deal with disciplinary matters — another area of co-operation which is still limited to a small number of countries.

When governments find it necessary to bring in policies of austerity in the public service, they should make sure that state employees continue to participate as before in determining their conditions of employment. This is the view of the ILO's Joint Committee on the Public Service. [54] The Committee has also observed that when a country receives assistance for its development, the conditions under which aid is given should not have a negative effect on conditions of employment in the public service or undermine participation by public servants in determining those conditions.

Two-way communication

Although it concerns all forms of business or industry, the ILO's Communications within the Undertaking Recommendation, 1967 (No. 129), [18] has meaning for schools, teachers and their employers. Information, rapidly disseminated and exchanged within the undertaking, helps to create mutual understanding and confidence, favours efficiency and is in the interests of the workers' aspirations, this Recommendation states.

Each enterprise should have a communications policy established after consultation with workers' representatives, to ensure the regular two-way communication of objective information between management and staff — especially before decisions are taken on questions of major interest to the staff. The methods used, however, should in no way weaken the principle of freedom of association or prejudice the activities of freely chosen workers' organisations or workers' representatives.

Various ways are proposed in Recommendation No. 129 to strengthen communication within an enterprise or service, with the choice to be made in line with the nature and size of the business, the composition and interests of its staff, and national practices. They include meetings, bulletins and personnel policy manuals, house journals, exhibitions, audio-visual media, and the means for the workers to submit their ideas on the running of the undertaking.

Dealing with grievances

Teachers should be protected against arbitrary action affecting their professional standing or career, in the words of the 1966 Recommendation, and the guide-lines given in ILO Recommendation No. 130 [19] on the examination of grievances can provide the necessary guarantees.

This ILO standard states that any worker who considers that he or she has a grievance should have the right — acting as an individual or jointly with others — to submit the problem, without suffering any prejudice, and have it examined under an appropriate procedure. The basis of the grievance may lie in relations between employer and worker, or the conditions of employment of one or several employees, when it seems that the situation is not in accordance with a collective agreement, an individual contract of employment, work rules, laws or regulations, custom or usage.

One of the principles laid down in Recommendation No. 130 is that the worker who complains should have the right to take part in the hearing of the grievance, and to be assisted or represented by a representative of a workers' organisation, by a workers' representative in the enterprise, or by anyone else he or she cares to choose.

The right to strike

Should teachers have the right to strike? The 1966 Recommendation proposes that joint machinery should be created for the settlement of disputes involving teachers and their employers. If all means of negotiation are exhausted or if there is a breakdown in the talks between the parties, teachers' organisations "should have the right to take such other steps as are normally open to other organisations in the defence of their legitimate interests".

For the past 20 years the Joint ILO/Unesco Committee of Experts on the Application of the Recommendation has interpreted this phrase as meaning that teachers should, indeed, have the right to strike, while drawing attention to the fact that for those teachers who are public servants — and they are in the great majority — ILO Convention No. 151 [31] makes the necessary provision for the settlement of disputes.

In general, the ILO's supervisory bodies have always maintained that going on strike is a basic means for workers and their organisations to promote and protect their economic and social interests.

Trade unions, in the view of the Committee of Experts on the Application of Conventions and Recommendations, should be able to stage protest strikes, in particular to express their opposition to a government's economic and social policies. Restrictions on working to rule, on the occupation of a firm or working premises, on sit-down strikes and picketing can only be justified if the action ceases to be peaceful.

Strikes of a purely political character, however, are not protected by the ILO's principles of freedom of association.

Indefinite restrictions on, or prohibitions of, the right to strike should not be regarded as justifiable unless they involve public servants who perform essential services of a kind that, if interrupted, would put at risk the lives, personal safety or health of all or part of the population. ILO bodies — in particular the Committee on Freedom of Association — do not consider that teachers are in this category.

Remuneration and working time 4

A practical way for teachers to measure their standing in the public eye is to compare their working conditions, pay and other material advantages with those of other professions.

The comparison may help to provide the answers to a number of questions. Is, for example, the work of teachers properly appreciated? Are they given due credit for qualifications and competence? What, in fact, is the status of teachers in society?

The fundamental importance of these questions is recognised in the International Covenant on Economic, Social and Cultural Rights, which forms part of the United Nations' International Bill of Human Rights. In spelling out the right of everyone to education, the Covenant states that "… the material conditions of teaching staff shall be continuously improved".

This concern underlies the 1966 Recommendation concerning the Status of Teachers. It is also evident in other international labour standards which can be applied to the teaching profession.

Two issues stand out in any consideration of working conditions: remuneration and working time. The international standards which cover these issues and their application to the teaching profession will be described in this chapter.

Remuneration

The 1966 Recommendation states that the standing of teachers and the degree of appreciation of what they do depend largely on their economic situation. Their salaries should:

— reflect the importance to society of teaching and of teachers and their responsibilities;
— compare favourably with salaries in other occupations requiring similar or equivalent qualifications;

— provide a reasonable standard of living for teachers and their families, as well as allowing them to improve their professional qualifications through further education or cultural activities; and

— take account of the fact that some posts call for higher qualifications and experience and carry greater responsibilities.

Teachers' pay, a study made by the ILO for the Joint ILO/Unesco Committee of Experts on the Application of the Recommendation,[42] points out that inadequate pay affects recruitment of teachers as well as the stability of the profession, creates frustrations which may lead to disruption of education, or even bring about a decline in professional standards; the negation, in fact, of one of the guiding principles of the 1966 Recommendation where it states that "working conditions for teachers should be such as will best promote effective learning and enable teachers to concentrate on their professional tasks".

Salary adjustments

Salary scales should be established in agreement with teachers' organisations, according to the 1966 Recommendation. It adds that scales should be reviewed periodically to take into account factors such as a rise in the cost of living, increased productivity leading to higher living standards in the country or a general upward movement in wage or salary levels.

Where salaries are indexed to the cost of living, teachers' organisations should participate in the choice of index for the profession; cost-of-living allowances should be treated as an integral part of earnings for pension purposes.

Consultation with teachers' organisations before the introduction of merit-rating systems of setting salaries is also proposed in the 1966 Recommendation.

Other points on remuneration made in the 1966 Recommendation include:

— basing salary differentials on objective criteria, such as levels of qualification, years of experience, or degrees of responsibility;

— advancement within the grade through salary increments granted at regular, preferably annual, intervals. Increments should be granted during probationary or temporary service;

— equal treatment for teachers on probation or employed on a temporary basis. Qualified teachers with either status should not be paid on a lower salary scale than that which applies to established staff; and

— allowance for the value of practical training and experience in the case of vocational or technical teachers without academic degrees when placed on a basic salary scale.

Three Conventions, each accompanied by a Recommendation, have been adopted by the ILO in the field of wages over the past 40 years. They are the Protection of Wages Convention, 1949 (No. 95), and Recommendation (No. 85),[5] the Equal Remuneration Convention, 1951 (No. 100), and Recommendation (No. 90),[7] and the Minimum Wage Fixing Convention, 1970 (No. 131), and Recommendation (No. 135).[21]

Protection of wages

Convention No. 95 requires wages to be paid fully, promptly and regularly in a manner that provides protection against abuse. It applies to all persons to whom wages are due. Under the Convention, deductions from wages shall only be permitted under conditions and to the extent prescribed by national legislation, collective agreements or arbitration awards.

Recommendation No. 85 specifies that deductions from wages for the reimbursement of loss or damage to the installations of the employer shall be authorised only if the worker can clearly be shown to be responsible, and the worker should be heard before such a deduction is made.

Remuneration without discrimination

Equal remuneration for men and women for work of equal value is established by Convention No. 100. All States which ratify this Convention — more than 100 have so far done so — agree to promote remuneration without discrimination based on sex.

The Convention defines remuneration as including basic wages or salaries and any additional payments — direct or indirect, in cash or in kind — by the employer to the worker in connection with his or her employment.

To apply the principle of equal remuneration, the Convention proposes national legislation, legal machinery, and collective agreements, or a combination of these means.

Jobs are to be evaluated, if this will help to apply the Convention.

Governments should co-operate with employers' and workers' organisations in putting the Convention into effect. Although the Convention implies that national authorities should observe the principle of equal remuneration in their own fields of competence, States are not obliged to make it generally applicable by writing it into national law. The accompanying Recommendation No. 90, however, proposes that the principle should be legally enacted, "where appropriate in the light of the methods in operation for the determination of rates of remuneration".

A survey of equal remuneration by the ILO's Committee of Experts on the Application of Conventions and Recommendations[53] came to the conclusion that the public authorities must play an active role. More and more governments, finding that encouragement and recommendations are not enough, have passed legislation to apply the principle of equal remuneration generally.

Many of the difficulties faced in achieving equal remuneration, the Committee notes, are linked to the general status of women and men in employment and in society. In the public sector — where the great majority of teachers are employed — discrimination results from sex bias in the criteria chosen for post classifications and the application of pay scales, inequalities in the payment of allowances and pensions, or to a disproportionate number of women in the lowest paid or in non-permanent categories.

When the equal remuneration instruments were being drawn up by the ILO, it was realised that measures to promote equality in this field went hand-in-hand with efforts to achieve parity between men and women workers in other areas.

For this reason, Recommendation No. 90 proposes a number of steps to make it easier to apply Convention No. 100. These are to:

— ensure that both sexes have equal or equivalent facilities for vocational guidance, training and placement and to encourage women to use them;

— provide welfare and social services to meet the needs of women who work, particularly those with family responsibilities; and

— promote equal access to occupations and posts.

These proposals have been developed and updated in other ILO instruments dealing with equality of opportunity and treatment which are mentioned earlier, in Chapter 2, Employment and career.

In addition, Recommendation No. 90 asks for efforts to promote public understanding of the principle of equal remuneration, for its application to all central government employees, and wherever the payment of staff is under statutory regulation or public control. Its application to local government employees, which is commonly the case of teachers, should also be encouraged.

Minimum wages

Instruments drafted with the needs of developing countries in mind, the Minimum Wage Fixing Convention, 1970 (No. 131), and Recommendation No. 135,[21] require ratifying States to establish a system of minimum wages covering all groups of wage earners (defined as workers in an employment relationship) where the terms of employment are such as to make coverage appropriate. The groups to be covered are to be determined either in agreement, or after consultation, with employers' and workers' organisations.

States must give the reason for not covering any of the groups excluded, and Recommendation No. 135 proposes that the number of wage earners not covered be kept to a minimum. The system, also according to the Recommendation, may consist of a single minimum wage or a series of minima for particular groups of workers.

The freedom of collective bargaining must be respected, particularly as a means of fixing wages above the minimum.

Two principal elements to be taken into account in determining the level of minimum wages should include:

— the needs of workers and their families, looking at factors such as the general level of wages in the country, the cost of living, social security benefits and the relative living standards of other social groups; and

— economic factors, taking into account the requirements of economic development, levels of productivity, and the desirability of achieving and maintaining a high level of employment.

Mechanisms are needed to fix and adjust minimum wages. Recommendation No. 135 offers a number of ways in which this may be done: by statute; decisions of a competent authority; decisions of wages boards or councils; of labour courts; or by giving collective agreements the force of law.

The Convention provides that in setting up, operating or modifying minimum wage fixing machinery there must be full consultation with the representative organisations of employers and workers; if the nature of the mechanism is appropriate, these organisations should participate on an equal footing in its work.

Minimum wages, under the Convention, are legally binding; failure to apply them makes anyone concerned liable to sanctions. Steps have to be taken — adequate inspection, for example — to ensure that all provisions concerning minimum wages are respected.

Pressures for change

In *Teachers' pay*, mentioned above, a general survey of public education in 70 countries gives information on the procedures for determining remuneration, pay differentials between different categories, the comparability of pay with other occupational groups, the different elements that make up teachers' remuneration and adjustments to the cost of living.

The survey, published in 1978, ends on a moderately optimistic note. The pressures for change in the consensus on the economic status of teachers which has evolved in different societies, it states, are due to a number of factors. These include changes in the concepts and techniques of teaching; growing awareness of the importance of education as a factor in national development and prosperity; the desire, expressed by many governments, to improve the status and economic condition of the profession; and the increasingly important role of teachers' organisations in determining the conditions of employment of their members.

Among other problems, one is to strike an acceptable compromise between the economic aspirations of the teaching profession and the ability of the community to satisfy those aspirations. "Increasingly often," concludes *Teachers' pay*, "the question is asked: can the country afford to pay? The question may equally well be asked: can the country afford not to pay?"

Reliable statistics

Social policy — covering remuneration and working time, as in other branches — is difficult to formulate and apply if sufficient and reliable statistics are not collected and compiled. The Joint ILO/Unesco Committee of Experts on the Application of the Recommendation concerning the Status of Teachers has repeatedly suggested that the statistical coverage of teachers be improved. There are ILO standards which provide guidance in this field, in particular the Labour Statistics Convention, 1985 (No. 160), and Recommendation (No. 170). [38]

Hours of work

In setting the number of hours teachers are required to work per day and per week, the 1966 Recommendation states that education authorities should consult the professional organisations. In many countries this does happen, with the teachers' organisations simply submitting suggestions in some cases, and in others taking part in negotiations. In a considerable number of countries, however, the authorities do not consult the organisations concerned.

Several factors should be taken into account in fixing hours of teaching, the 1966 Recommendation suggests. They include:

— the number of pupils with whom the teacher is required to work per day and per week;
— the need for time to plan and prepare lessons and evaluate work;
— the number of different lessons to be taught each day;
— the demands on the teacher of research, co-curricular and extra-curricular activities, supervision and counselling of pupils; and
— time to report to, and consult with, parents.

Normal hours of teaching should be reduced, the Recommendation continues, if teachers are assigned to special educational responsibilities in addition to classroom instruction. Time should be allowed for teachers to take part in in-service training programmes. Extra-curricular activities should not be allowed to become excessive nor to interfere with a teacher's main duties. However, the 1966 Recommendation does call on teachers to take part in these activities, thus assuming a dynamic role in developing education and community work outside the framework of the school.

These issues were addressed by the ILO Joint Meeting on Conditions of Work of Teachers [45] in 1981. The Joint Meeting drew attention to the increasing workload of teachers as a result of the demands made by some societies on their educational systems.

Classroom hours have remained stable, but the time needed to prepare lessons, mark papers and to do work ancillary to teaching has expanded, the Joint Meeting noted. Counselling and guidance, meetings with parents, course development and — in developing countries — national development activities, have become part of the functions of many teachers. When is the additional work done? Often at home in the evenings, at weekends or during school holidays.

The Joint Meeting warned that excessive working hours affect the teacher's ability to give of his or her best in the classroom. For this reason, governments should try to determine the actual average weekly working hours of teachers, in consultation with the professional organisations. Maximum normal working hours should be set on the basis of these inquiries at levels which do not put an excessive burden on teachers and do not prejudice the carrying out of their main duties.

Another conclusion of the Joint Meeting was that the normal hours of teaching of newcomers to the profession should be set below the generally applied standards in an introductory period, because they need more time to prepare and evaluate their lessons. Older teachers should also have the possibility of working reduced hours — at their request — as a means of easing pressures as the age of retirement approaches.

The effect of educational innovations on teachers' total hours of work should be carefully monitored, the Joint Meeting added.

Reduction of hours of work

Setting the 40-hour week without a cut in wages as the goal, the Reduction of Hours of Work Recommendation, 1962 (No. 116),[13] proposes that each member State, consistent with national conditions and practice, should apply the principle of the progressive reduction of normal hours of work.

Where the normal working week exceeds 48 hours, steps should be taken immediately to bring it down to 40 hours, without reducing wages.

"Normal hours" are defined in Recommendation No. 116 as the number of hours fixed by laws, regulations, collective agreements or arbitration awards. Where working time is not fixed by these means, "normal" represents the number of hours beyond which overtime is paid, or which constitute an exception to recognised rules or customs.

Ways of achieving the 40-hour week are to be worked out and put into practice according to national circumstances and conditions in each branch of economic activity, taking into account the level of economic development, progress in raising productivity through modern technology and management techniques, and the preferences of employers' and workers' organisations.

Priority should be given, Recommendation No. 116 continues, to industries and occupations that involve heavy physical or mental strain or health risks for the workers concerned, particularly where they consist mainly of women or young persons.

The limits to the total number of hours of overtime that can be worked in a given period should also be established by the competent authorities. In arranging overtime, the special circumstances of young persons, pregnant women, nursing mothers and the handicapped should be taken into account.

Recommendation No. 116 provides for the enforcement of measures to reduce hours of work, including inspection, and for sanctions for non-observance.

Holidays and leave

Teachers should enjoy the right to an adequate annual vacation with pay.

The Joint ILO/Unesco Committee of Experts on the Application of the Recommendation concerning the Status of Teachers emphasises that this part of the 1966 Recommendation should not be confused with "school holidays", which are given over in part to compulsory activities: training, preparation for the following year's classes, administrative duties and remedial classes.

These activities should not take up so much time that teachers have shorter holidays than those granted to other workers. Established teachers in the public sector, the Committee notes, do not seem to have problems over remuneration during their holidays; those who are not in full employment or who are in private schools are not always paid in full at vacation time, and this is a matter for concern.

The Holidays with Pay Convention (Revised), 1970 (No. 132), [22] applies to all employed persons, except seafarers, but some of the 19 ratifying States have exercised an option to exclude limited categories — in some cases, public servants. The Convention fixes a minimum annual paid holiday of three weeks for one year of service. A State may specify a longer holiday when it ratifies the Convention or by a later declaration.

For less than one year's service, a holiday with pay of proportionate length must be granted, but a minimum period not exceeding six months may be required for any paid holiday entitlement.

The division of the annual holiday into parts may be authorised by the competent authority or through the appropriate machinery. However, one of the parts must consist of two uninterrupted working weeks, unless otherwise provided in an agreement applicable to both employer and employee.

The uninterrupted part of the holiday must be taken no later than one year, and the remainder no later than 18 months, from the end of the year in which the entitlement arises.

At what time of year should holidays be taken? The Convention provides that this shall be decided by the employer after consultation with the employee or his or her representative, unless the period is already fixed by regulation, collective agreement, arbitration award or some other means; the requirements of work on the one hand and the opportunities for rest and relaxation that the employee can enjoy on the other, are to be taken into account.

There may be special rules for cases where the employed person works for gain during an annual break, if this conflicts with the purpose of the holiday.

Agreements to give up the right to annual holiday with pay, or to renounce it in favour of compensation or otherwise are null, void or prohibited under Convention No. 132.

A State which ratifies the Convention must give effect to its provisions in national laws and regulations to the extent that it is not applied by collective agreements, arbitration awards, court decisions, statutory wage-fixing machinery or other means suited to national conditions. There must be ways — adequate inspection, for example — to ensure that national regulations or other means of implementing the Convention are enforced.

The entire field of working time, the reduction of hours of work, weekly rest and holidays with pay has been surveyed by the ILO's Committee of Experts on the Application of Conventions and Recommendations, in a report to the International Labour Conference. [48] The survey examines national law and practice in the light of the principal ILO instruments.

Sick leave

Teachers, in the terms of the 1966 Recommendation, are entitled to sick leave with pay. In establishing the period during which full or partial pay is granted, allowance should be made for cases in which teachers have to be isolated from pupils for long periods.

Educational leave

In proposing that teachers should be granted study leave on full or partial pay at intervals, the 1966 Recommendation was ahead of the ILO itself. The International Labour Conference recognised the importance of this type of leave by adopting the Paid Educational Leave Convention, 1974 (No. 140), and Recommendation (No. 148). [26]

The 1966 Recommendation also states that periods of study should be counted for seniority and pension purposes, and that teachers in remote areas should be granted study leave more frequently.

In a large number of countries teachers are entitled to take study leave from time to time on full or partial salary — depending on the nature and purpose of the leave. In some countries, however, study leave — or certain types of study leave — is taken without pay. There are also cases where the period of leave does not count for seniority or pension. Only a few countries give study leave more frequently to teachers in remote areas.

Convention No. 140 requires States which ratify it to draw up and apply a policy which promotes the granting of paid educational leave. This is defined as leave granted to a worker for educational purposes for a specified period during working hours "with adequate financial entitlements".

Paid educational leave, in the terms of the Convention, counts as part of service for the purpose of establishing claims to social benefits and other employment rights.

According to Recommendation No. 148, the earnings of workers on educational leave should be maintained by payment of their wages and other benefits, or by adequate compensation. Major additional costs of education or training should be taken into account.

Paid educational leave covers training at all levels, social and civic education, and trade union education, in the terms offered by Recommendation No. 148. It is designed to contribute to:

— continuing education and training in general;
— employment and job security in conditions of scientific and technological development and economic and structural change; and
— participation of workers and their representatives in the life of the undertaking and of the community.

A national policy for the promotion of paid educational leave should be co-ordinated with policies for employment, education and training, as well as with those concerning hours of work, according to Recommendation No. 148. There should be special provision for certain types of undertakings and categories of workers, the latter including those with family responsibilities or living in isolated areas.

To assure regular and adequate financing for paid educational leave, the Recommendation proposes contributions — according to their responsibilities — from employers, public authorities, educational and training institutions, and employers' and workers' organisations.

The efficient continuing operation of undertakings is ensured if the manner in which workers are granted educational leave is agreed between the enterprise or service concerned (or employers' organisations) and workers' organisations. When leave is granted for trade union education, the selection of candidates should be the responsibility of the workers' organisations, the Recommendation adds.

When Convention No. 140 and Recommendation No. 148 were adopted in 1974, the International Labour Conference at the same time passed a resolution to ensure co-ordination between the ILO and other international organisations — particularly Unesco — on the question of paid educational leave.

Health and safety   5

All types of undertakings, public or private, have a range of risks to health and safety. Schools are no exception to the rule. For this reason, the ILO's standards covering occupational safety and health are as much the concern of education authorities, the teaching profession and school pupils as they are for the people who own, manage and work in offices and factories.

Since it was established after the First World War, the ILO has been the basic international source of reference on the health and safety of workers. Apart from setting standards which serve as a model for national legislation and practice throughout the world, the ILO has helped to create or upgrade occupational safety and health services in a number of countries.

In every region of the world, management training, vocational education, vocational rehabilitation and social security systems bear the imprint of ILO technical co-operation. Wherever the ILO has been called upon to provide assistance in these fields, it has, as a matter of course, introduced sound occupational safety and health practices.

This is the background to the following account of ILO health and safety standards as they concern education authorities, school managers and the teaching profession.

The 1966 Recommendation concerning the Status of Teachers [1] refers to health and safety issues, but the main texts are the ILO's Occupational Safety and Health Convention, 1981 (No. 155), its accompanying Recommendation (No. 164), [34] the Occupational Health Services Convention, 1985 (No. 161), and its accompanying Recommendation No. 171. [39]

Comprehensive approach

Convention No. 155 marks a new departure for the ILO. In contrast to previous action which focused on specific occupational safety or health needs, the new Convention is comprehensive and applies to all activities and all workers — including the public service. The accent is on a "coherent national policy" on occupational safety, occupational health and the working environment. The aim of the policy should be the prevention of accidents and injury to health linked to work by reducing the causes of hazards in the working environment.

The Convention defines the main spheres of action under such a policy. It provides detailed proposals for action at the national level and at the level of the undertaking. The standard deals with the adaptation of equipment, working time, organisation of work and processes to the physical and mental capacities of workers.

Communication and co-operation at all levels, and the qualifications and motivation of persons involved in the process of ensuring adequate levels of safety and health, are also subjects of Convention No. 155.

"Health" in relation to work is not merely the absence of disease or infirmity; the Convention is based on the concept of well-being as it relates to safety and health at work.

The Convention states that questions of occupational safety and health should be a part of education and training, including higher technical, medical and professional education. It can be inferred that teacher training is included.

Consultation

Convention No. 155 places emphasis on consultation. Workers, their representatives or their organisations should be able to inquire into all aspects of safety and health associated with their work, and be consulted on these issues by their employers. The accompanying Recommendation No. 164 proposes the appointment of workers' safety delegates and workers' or joint management/worker safety and health committees. It also draws attention to the responsibility of workers to take reasonable care of their own safety and that of others who may be affected by what they do — or fail to do — at the workplace.

Occupational health services

The Occupational Health Services Convention, 1985 (No. 161), and its accompanying Recommendation (No. 171),[39] go a step further. States which ratify this Convention undertake to develop occupational health services for all workers — the public service is included — in consultation with employers' and workers' organisations.

Designed to establish and maintain a safe and healthy working environment in one or a number of undertakings, each occupational health service should be multidisciplinary in its staffing and duties.

The tasks foreseen for such services include the identification and assessment of risks, monitoring of premises and of workers' health, giving advice on the planning and organisation of work, contributing to the improvement of working practices and the testing of new equipment, participating in training, education and vocational rehabilitation, the organisation of first aid, and the analysis of occupational accidents and diseases.

Some of the concerns of developing countries and of all places where remoteness poses problems are addressed in Recommendation No. 171. The Recommendation, for example, suggests that occupational health services might also carry out immunisations, and offer curative medical care for workers and their families who live at a distance from regular medical services.

The Recommendation also proposes that where undertakings are unable to set up an occupational health service, arrangements should be made with a local medical service to carry out health examinations, monitor the health situation, and ensure that first aid and emergency treatment facilities are properly organised.

Well-being: The basic requirements

Without satisfactory working conditions, the well-being of teachers is at risk. The 1966 Recommendation concerning the Status of Teachers adopts the guiding principle that working conditions should be "such as will best promote effective learning and enable teachers to concentrate on their professional tasks".

In setting out the conditions for effective teaching and learning, the 1966 Recommendation is dealing with questions which have an obvious bearing on health and safety. The size of classes, it states, should permit teachers to give individual attention to pupils; ancillary staff should be appointed for non-teaching duties to enable teachers to concentrate on their professional tasks.

Working hours, per day and per week, should be established in consultation with teachers' organisations. In fixing the number of hours, the number of pupils, the need to find time for planning and preparation of lessons and evaluation of work, the number of lessons to be taught each day, and the other demands on a teacher's time — research, extra-curricular activities, supervisory duties and pupil counselling, for example — should all be taken into account. Teachers also need time to report to, and consult with, parents, as well as for in-service training.

On the other hand, extra-curricular activities should not be allowed to interfere with a teacher's main duties. Those with special educational responsibilities outside the classroom should have their normal hours of teaching correspondingly reduced.

The Occupational Safety and Health Recommendation, 1981 (No. 164), takes up the theme when it refers in similar terms to the responsibility of all employers to create safe and healthy conditions of work. It notes the obligation "to take all reasonably practicable measures with a view to eliminating excessive physical and mental fatigue" and to ensure that the organisation of work in terms of hours and rest breaks does not adversely affect occupational safety and health.

Stress

More than ever in the past, stress — its effects on the health of teachers and the quality of the education they provide — is causing concern in many countries.

Parents and society in general are demanding more of education systems, bringing a corresponding increase in the workload of teaching staff. The changes in many branches of education have been rapid and unceasing in recent years. To these factors of strain, others can be added:

— inclusion in ordinary classes of pupils with different national, linguistic or cultural backgrounds or children with learning difficulties or with special needs;

— excessive working hours, oversize classes, too few teachers in proportion to the numbers of pupils;

— poor working conditions, inadequate buildings and/or equipment;
— lack of consultation of teachers by management before decisions are taken;
— sense of isolation, common to all teachers when facing their classes;
— for teachers with family responsibilities, the dual burden of a job and managing a household; and
— keeping discipline and dealing with violence, drugs and other social problems, especially in classes where pupils see no benefit in staying on at school.

ILO proposals

The problem of stress came to the forefront at the ILO's Joint Meeting on Conditions of Work of Teachers [45] in 1981, which brought together representatives of governments and of the teaching profession. This meeting made a series of proposals to deal with situations in which teachers are under pressures which may affect their health or professional capacity. (The issue is also raised in ILO Recommendation No. 164 when it speaks of "prevention of harmful physical or mental stress due to conditions of work" as a field of action in occupational safety and health).

Where pupils with special needs are kept in regular classes, the Joint Meeting concluded, special teaching assistance may be provided. As an alternative, the factors generating stress may be removed. Disabled children, those with different national, linguistic or cultural backgrounds or the disruptive elements may, for example, be given all or part of their schooling in special classes until they come close enough to general school or class standards to be reintegrated.

The meeting agreed that checking disruptive behaviour and acts of violence against teachers calls for:

— closer association of pupils, teachers and parents in the functioning of schools, to promote a sense of responsibility;
— official campaigns to gain public support for teachers and the aims of education;
— agreement between education authorities and teachers' organisations on disciplinary measures, which would be publicised and strictly carried out;
— rapid access to legal assistance and guarantees of compensation for teachers who are victims of violence;
— promotion of better understanding between pupils and teachers, for example by creating joint school committees; and
— recognising the value of smaller classes.

In a number of other conclusions, the Joint Meeting stated that:

— training and retraining programmes should help teachers to cope with stress factors, while the feeling of isolation can sometimes be overcome by team teaching arrangements and advisory services;

— the selection process for new teachers should take account of motivation, adaptability and general suitability;

— in the course of periodic medical check-ups for teachers, the examiner should look for signs of stress. Teachers whose health is already affected in this way should have therapeutic help and access to retraining;

— as a means of reducing stress, the teaching hours of new entrants and of older teachers should be shortened; and

— schools should have rest and leisure facilities for the staff — a proposal made for all workers in the Welfare Facilities Recommendation, 1956 (No. 102),[9] which deals as well with the provision of canteens and transport to and from work where public transport is not available.

The problem of stress among older workers, who may be taken to include senior teachers, is dealt with in the Older Workers' Recommendation, 1980 (No. 162).[32] This instrument proposes among other things that:

— the normal daily and weekly hours of work of older workers employed on arduous, hazardous or unhealthy work should be reduced;

— when they ask for it, older workers should be granted a gradual reduction of working hours over a prescribed period before reaching the age when they qualify for an old-age benefit;

— annual paid holidays should be increased on the basis of length of service or age; and

— older workers should be given the possibility to organise their work time and leisure to suit their convenience, particularly through part-time employment and flexible hours.

The importance of the stress issue was again underlined by the Joint ILO/Unesco Committee of Experts on the Application of the Recommendation at its 1988 meeting: the Joint Committee requested the ILO to put the issue of stress and its impact on teachers and the profession on its future research agenda as a priority work item.

Living conditions

Problems which affect the entire profession often bear more severely on teachers in rural and isolated regions, although it is now realised that those who work in the poor areas of city centres may be just as much at a disadvantage, and should have at least some of the same consideration.

Aside from the questions of pay and career prospects, living conditions are often an acute concern for these teachers, and may have an adverse affect on their health and professional capacities.

For these reasons, the 1966 Recommendation proposes that decent housing, free or with a subsidised rent, should be provided for teachers and their families in areas remote from population centres. In countries where teachers are expected, in addition to their normal duties, to stimulate community activities, accommodation should be provided for in development plans.

These proposals bring to the situation of teachers the main points of the Workers' Housing Recommendation, 1961 (No. 115), [12] which calls for a national housing policy aimed at providing adequate and decent accommodation and a suitable living environment for all workers and their families, with priority to those whose needs are most urgent.

The 1966 Recommendation also calls for removal and travel expenses on transfer to remote areas, as well as for annual leave, and for travel facilities for teachers to maintain their professional standards.

The 1981 Joint Meeting on Conditions of Work of Teachers went further in proposing special attention to housing for women teachers, particularly those with small children.

Medical care

Periodic, free medical examinations are a recognised principle of occupational safety and health, and all teachers, in the view of the authors of the 1966 Recommendation, should undergo them. In addition, provision should be made for medical care and other benefits with a view to restoring or at least improving the health of disabled teachers, as well as for rehabilitation services to prepare them for a return to their previous activity.

In places where medical facilities are scarce, teachers should be paid expenses to travel to obtain appropriate care.

The Joint Meeting on Conditions of Work of Teachers also addressed the question. It concluded that measures should be taken to safeguard the health of teachers. They should have adequate medical care facilities as well as periodic examinations.

Building and functioning of schools

The concept and the quality of buildings is a vital factor in ensuring the health and safety of those who will use them. For this reason, the 1966 Recommendation on the Status of Teachers made the general comment that school buildings must be safe and attractive in overall design and functional in layout. They should be constructed in accordance with accepted sanitary standards, be durable, adaptable and easy to maintain.

The 1966 Recommendation adds that it is the responsibility of the authorities to see that school premises are properly maintained so as not to threaten in any way the health and safety of pupils and teachers.

In these proposals, the 1966 Recommendation anticipates the Occupational Safety and Health Convention, 1981 (No. 155), which requires employers to ensure that workplaces, machinery, equipment and processes under their control are safe and without risk to health.

The Convention also states that chemical, physical and biological substances and agents should be without risk to health when the correct protective measures are taken. Protective clothing and equipment should be provided to avoid the risk of accidents or danger to health. There should be the means of dealing with emergencies and accidents, including first-aid arrangements.

Detailed, technical ways of meeting the requirements of Convention No. 155 are spelled out in the accompanying Recommendation No. 164.

Laboratories and vocational training workshops first come to mind in reading these articles of the Convention, but it requires little reflection to realise that they have a much more general application to the design and use of school buildings.

The 1966 Recommendation states that, when new schools are being planned, representative teacher opinion should be taken into account and the staff should be consulted when additional accommodation is being planned for an existing school. These forms of consultation are still far from universal.

Participation of teachers or their representatives in drawing up health and safety standards for schools was urged by the 1981 Joint Meeting on Conditions of Work of Teachers. The Joint Meeting took the position that badly designed, low-standard buildings in terms of space, ventilation, sanitation, and acoustics are generators of stress for pupils and teachers. These factors, as well as heating, lighting, structural safety, fire hazards and durability should be taken into account in establishing standards.

Use of asbestos

A very precise danger to health in workplaces is the use of asbestos as a construction material or for insulation — and it has often been employed in the past in building schools. The Asbestos Convention, 1986 (No. 162), and Recommendation (No. 172), [40] require exposure to asbestos to be prevented or controlled by proper engineering techniques and work practices.

The Convention and Recommendation propose the use of less harmful materials and techniques, and call for a ban on all asbestos spraying and on the use of a particularly dangerous form: crocidolite. The responsibilities of employers are outlined, as well as the precautions to be taken in demolishing buildings containing asbestos insulation, in the removal of asbestos which is likely to become airborne, and in the disposal of asbestos waste.

Other ILO standards

Certain standards adopted by the ILO to provide protection against specific risks since the 1966 Recommendation concerning the Status of Teachers have not been mentioned elsewhere in this chapter. These instruments nevertheless have an interest for the teaching profession and are listed below. They affect, in particular, teachers who work in laboratories, workshops, and technical and vocational schools:

— the Guarding of Machinery Convention, 1963 (No. 119), and Recommendation (No. 118); the Maximum Weight Convention, 1967 (No. 127), and Recommendation (No. 128); [14]

— the Benzene Convention, 1971 (No. 136), and Recommendation (No. 144); [24]

— the Occupational Cancer Convention, 1974 (No. 139), and Recommendation (No. 147); [25] and

— the Working Environment (Air Pollution, Noise and Vibration) Convention, 1977 (No. 148), and Recommendation (No. 156). [29]

Safety and health are also touched on in the Labour Administration Convention, 1978 (No. 150), and Recommendation (No. 158). [30]

Social security 6

Teachers are rarely covered by specific social security schemes; in most cases they are included in arrangements which cater for the needs of public servants or for workers in general.

The social security rights of the profession have nevertheless been set out in the 1966 Recommendation concerning the Status of Teachers, [1] which in turn takes its inspiration from a number of international labour standards adopted by the ILO.

Social security for teachers, [43] a study made by the ILO at the request of the Joint ILO/Unesco Committee of Experts on the Application of the Recommendation, and published in 1979, examines the extent to which the Recommendation's provisions are applied and the application of ILO social security instruments to teachers. Other sources of reference are a general survey of social security protection in old age [57] by the ILO's Committee of Experts on the Application of Conventions and Recommendations, the ILO publication *Introduction to social security*, [49] and Report III of the ILO's Joint Committee on the Public Service, Fourth Session, 1988. [58]

The 1966 Recommendation states that all teachers, regardless of the type of school in which they serve, should enjoy the same or similar social security protection. Student teachers and those on probation are included, and the Recommendation is addressed, as always, to private schools as well as to those in the public sector.

The forms of social security which should protect teachers are those laid down in the Social Security (Minimum Standards) Convention, 1952 (No. 102), [8] namely medical care and benefits covering sickness, unemployment, old age, employment injury, family, maternity, invalidity and survivors.

In order to ratify this Convention, a country must accept three of the nine branches of social security benefits listed above, including at least one of the following: unemployment, employment injury, old-age, invalidity, or survivors' benefits.

The standards of social security provided for teachers should be at least as favourable as those set out in this Convention and in other ILO instruments, the 1966 Recommendation adds. (A number of Conventions and Recommendations in the field of social security have been adopted by the ILO since 1966 and these, too, serve as yardsticks in determining the rights of teachers.) Where benefits under a general scheme are below those recommended in the ILO instruments, they should be brought up to that level by supplementary measures.

Special factors

The 1966 Recommendation makes an original contribution in linking the protection of teachers to the special characteristics of the profession — a factor not always taken into account, since large numbers of teachers are covered by general social security schemes.

However, the 1966 Recommendation does not suggest that special schemes should be set up for the profession simply in the interests of harmonising protection among various categories of teachers or because the particular conditions of teaching should be taken into account.

It points out, on the contrary, that as far as possible the social security protection of teachers should be assured through a general scheme covering employed persons in the public sector or in the private sector as appropriate. Special arrangements should be considered only where there is no general scheme for a contingency covered in the Recommendation.

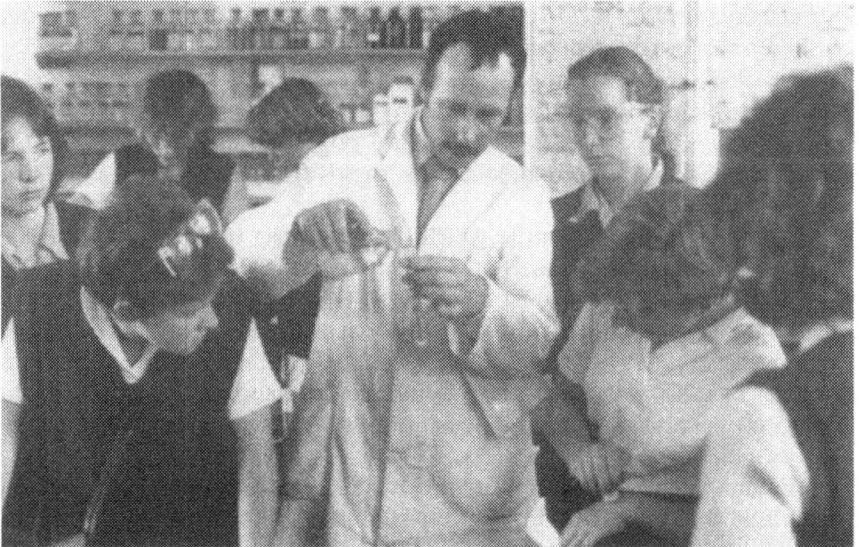

Among teachers' particular concerns in the field of social security which have been singled out by the Recommendation are:
— scarcity of medical facilities in some areas;
— longer absence in case of sickness to isolate teachers from pupils;
— accidents when teachers are engaged in school activities away from school premises or grounds;
— exposure to infectious diseases among children;
— transfers between authorities with different social security schemes;
— service beyond pensionable age to make up for a shortage of teachers; and
— demands on mental capacities.

Although Convention No. 102 is seen as an attainable objective for developing countries — flexibly drafted, it allows for temporary exceptions for countries "whose economy and medical facilities are insufficiently developed" — it is doubtful that any country can claim to have reached all the goals set in this and other ILO instruments dealing with social security.

In the great majority of countries the best coverage for teachers is provided in the form of old-age and sickness benefits, and the least in dealing with the contingency of unemployment and in providing for family responsibilities.

Pioneering legislation

Before outlining the implications for the teaching profession of each category of benefit in the light of the 1966 Recommendation and various ILO social security instruments, some of the characteristics of Convention No. 102 deserve to be mentioned.

The Convention:
— defines each type of contingency;
— sets out the minimum percentages of employees, the active population or all residents to be covered; and
— lays down the level and duration of a benefit and the conditions under which it is to be granted.

The Convention broke new ground by fixing the minimum amounts of benefits in periodic payments as a percentage of wages for each contingency covered.

Those provisions of the Convention, which are common to all branches of social security, cover adjustments in the level of pensions as a result of changes in the cost of living, equality of treatment of non-national residents, cases in which benefits may be suspended, the right of appeal against refusal of a benefit, and financing.

Under the Convention, the State accepts general responsibility for the administration of social security, whatever the arrangements made for its management.

Since the adoption of Convention No. 102 in 1952, the ILO has set higher standards of protection in the various branches of social security in a series of instruments which will be cited under different headings in this chapter. Most of these Conventions and Recommendations have been adopted since the preparation of the 1966 Recommendation concerning the Status of Teachers.

Medical care and sickness benefits

Medical care of a curative or preventive nature and sickness involving inca-pacity for work and a suspension of earnings are separate subjects dealt with in one instrument: the Medical Care and Sickness Benefits Convention, 1969 (No. 130). [20] Any State ratifying this Convention must accept both sets of obli-gations, but lower standards are permitted for countries where the economy and medical facilities are not well enough developed.

Casual workers may be excluded — and also public servants if they are pro-tected by special schemes providing benefits at least equivalent to those in the Convention.

Medical care under the Convention is given to maintain, restore or improve the health of the person protected and his or her ability to work and to attend to personal needs. It covers the services of general practitioners and special-ists, pharmaceutical supplies, hospitalisation, dental care and medical rehabili-tation.

The choice is offered of protecting all employees, including apprentices, and their wives and children; not less than 75 per cent of the active population; or not less than 75 per cent of all residents. As a rule, medical care must be provided for as long as it is needed.

A special requirement in the case of teachers is noted in the 1966 Recom-mendation. This is that teachers working in regions where medical facilities are scarce should be paid travelling expenses to obtain the care they need.

Maternity

Medical care in pregnancy and confinement shall include at least the ser-vices of medical practitioners or qualified midwives and hospitalisation when necessary, in the terms of Convention No. 102. This instrument, and two others — the Maternity Protection Convention, 1919 (No. 3), and the Maternity Protection Convention (Revised), 1952 (No. 103),[2] — all provide for 12 weeks' maternity leave. Convention No. 103 specifies that at least six weeks of maternity leave should be taken after confinement.

Women absent from work on maternity leave, according to Convention No. 103, should be entitled to cash and medical benefits. Cash benefits should amount to not less than two-thirds of the woman's previous earnings — but in no case should the employer be liable for the cost.

All countries have been asked in the 1966 Recommendation to put these ILO standards into current practice. In some countries maternity leave is granted without pay, and in certain cases social security benefits cover all or part of the salary.

The 1966 Recommendation also states that women should be encouraged to remain in service by the offer of additional unpaid leave of up to one year after childbirth without loss of employment or rights.

It is the practice in some countries to allow additional unpaid leave after the birth of a child — or even after adoption — for a period of years. Some countries reduce the number of hours of teaching for mothers, make it possible for them to serve part time, or grant additional leave days. In maternity, teachers' rights seem to be generally protected. However, the concept of parental leave is today tending to replace that of leave for the mother only.

Sickness benefit

Protection in this category extends to all employees, including apprentices; or not less than 75 per cent of the economically active population; or all residents whose means do not exceed a level prescribed in Convention No. 102. There must be periodic payments, calculated as 60 per cent of the total of family allowances and previous earnings of the beneficiary; or the wages of an ordinary adult male labourer, if a flat-rate formula is preferred.

Cash payments under the Convention may be limited to not less than 52 weeks, and may not be paid for up to three days after the suspension of earnings. The 1966 Recommendation sets a higher target for teachers, calling for payment from the first day of suspension of earnings and throughout the period of incapacity.

Payment throughout the period of incapacity is also proposed in Recommendation No. 134, which accompanies the above-mentioned Convention No. 130. This Recommendation goes further in providing that a person suffering a loss of earnings due to absence from work for curative or preventive care, convalescence or quarantine should receive a cash benefit.

The question of the need to isolate teachers from pupils (in cases of contagious diseases) arises in the 1966 Recommendation, which proposes an extension to the period of sickness benefit, if necessary, in such cases.

Convention No. 102 specifies that sickness benefits must be financed collectively by means of contributions or taxes. However, the labour legislation of many countries makes the employer directly responsible for these payments — a system which does not provide sufficient guarantees for workers in the private sector, and which may lead to financial difficulties for employers.

Employment injury

If, as a result of an industrial accident or occupational disease, a person is unable to work temporarily, becomes likely to lose permanently all or a substantial part of his or her earnings, or dies, leaving survivors without support, a periodic benefit is to be paid under the terms of the Employment Injury Benefits Convention, 1964 (No. 121). [15] The benefit is calculated as 60 per cent of the total of family allowances and previous earnings or, alternatively, as the wage of an adult wage labourer on a flat-rate basis. If the breadwinner dies, the percentage is 50 per cent.

Convention No. 121 sets higher standards than Convention No. 102, but it offers less rigorous options in favour of developing countries. Virtually all employees, including apprentices, are protected; the exceptions permitted, as in the case of Convention No. 130 (medical care and sickness benefits), are casual workers and public servants — if the latter are as well or better protected.

Protection of teachers

Each ratifying State must define an "industrial accident" but, in the terms of Recommendation No. 121, which accompanies Convention No. 121, the definition should include accidents, regardless of their cause, sustained during working hours at or near the place of work, or at any place where the worker would not have been except for his or her employment.

This meets a concern in the 1966 Recommendation: that teachers should be protected against injuries suffered when they are engaged in school activities away from school premises and grounds.

Infectious diseases prevalent among children should be considered as occupational diseases if contracted by teachers, the 1966 Recommendation states. The list of diseases attached to Convention No. 121, as revised in 1980, includes infectious diseases contracted in an occupation and from work where contamination is a risk, particularly in laboratories.

The problem of stress

Stress, described in the preceding chapter on health and safety, is not included in the list, although it is perhaps the most common occupational disease among teachers. When the International Labour Conference amended the list of occupational diseases in 1980 it noted, however, that diseases due to stress were among the hazards which might be considered for inclusion later. States which use a general definition of occupational diseases are at liberty to include stress if they wish.

Medical care is also featured in Convention No. 121. At the workplace there should be the means of emergency treatment for persons who have had a serious accident, and also follow-up care for slight injuries which do not entail stopping work.

States which ratify the Convention — apart from taking action to prevent injuries at work — are required to provide rehabilitation services.

In dealing with invalidity benefits for teachers, the 1966 Recommendation sets similar objectives. However, ILO Recommendation No. 121 proposes higher standards of benefits and coverage. It recommends, for example, the extension of benefits to the self-employed and to certain categories of persons working without pay, including students and school pupils.

Unemployment

The Employment Promotion and Protection against Unemployment Convention, 1988 (No. 168), and its accompanying Recommendation (No. 176)[41] are the most recent in a long line of ILO instruments, stretching back to the 1930s, which deal with the various aspects of employment policy, unemployment and underemployment.

A key provision of Convention No. 168 is that systems of protection against unemployment, in particular the methods of providing unemployment benefit, should contribute to the promotion of full, productive and freely chosen employment and not discourage employers from offering, and workers from seeking, productive jobs.

States which ratify the Convention undertake to provide support for those who are involuntarily unemployed. (Full unemployment is defined as the loss of earnings by a person who cannot find a suitable job, although capable of working, available, and looking for employment.)

In addition, States are asked to try to extend the protection of the Convention to cover loss of earnings due to partial unemployment — defined as a temporary reduction in the normal or statutory hours of work — and to situations where, without any break in employment, earnings are suspended or reduced as a result of a temporary halt of production. They should also try to pay benefits to part-time workers who are looking for full-time work.

Extent of coverage

At least 85 per cent of all employees, including apprentices, must be protected, but some public employees — those whose employment is guaranteed up to the normal retiring age — may be excluded. (This provision echoes the call in the 1966 Recommendation for social security coverage of probationers and trainees. Teachers who are public servants may enjoy life tenure once they are established, but there is always the possibility that they may not be permanently employed after their probationary period.)

In another provision, Convention No. 168 specifies that ratifying States may temporarily lower standards in a number of respects, including the size of the population covered.

Workers who are fully unemployed or laid off must, according to the Convention, be paid:

— not less than 50 per cent of their previous earnings; or

— 50 per cent of the statutory minimum wage; or

— 50 per cent of the wage of an ordinary labourer; or

— at a level which provides the minimum essential for basic living expenses,

whichever is the highest.

The qualifying period must not exceed the length deemed to be the minimum necessary to prevent abuse.

In cases of full unemployment, the waiting period before the benefit is paid must not exceed seven days, and the duration of full payments may be limited to 26 weeks in each spell without work, or to 39 weeks over any period of 24 months.

If unemployment continues beyond this period, further payments may be limited to a period set by national legislation, and may be adjusted to the means of the beneficiaries and their families.

Target for developing countries

In Convention No. 168, and in the practice of most of the industrialised countries, the levels of unemployment benefit laid down in 1952 in Convention No. 102 have been surpassed, but the latter are still useful as a target for developing countries that are able to set up an unemployment compensation scheme.

Convention No. 168 takes account of the fact that many people looking for work have never been covered by schemes for the protection of the unemployed — or have ceased to be protected. Ten categories of jobseekers in this situation — including young persons who have completed their studies, people who were previously self-employed, or who have had to stop work to bring up a child or to look after someone who is sick, disabled or elderly — are listed. Countries which have ratified the Convention must set social benefits for at least three of these categories.

However, a State may, by a declaration, exclude this part of the Convention from its obligations.

Partial unemployment

Benefits that should be paid in the case of partial unemployment and involuntary part-time work are not specified in Convention No. 168. These are dealt with in Recommendation No. 176, which proposes periodic payments, offering fair compensation for loss of earnings without setting a percentage target. The total of the benefit and earnings from part-time work, the Recommendation suggests, should lie between the amount of the previous earnings from full-time work and the full unemployment benefit.

A point which Convention No. 168 does make — and which also features in the 1966 Recommendation concerning the Status of Teachers — is that social security schemes should be adjusted to the circumstances of part-time workers. Recommendation No. 176 specifies areas where adjustments might be needed, including the minimum hours of work or of earnings necessary to become entitled to benefits, and the methods of calculating cash benefits, particularly pensions.

Invalidity, old-age and survivors' benefits

All three types of pension are covered in two ILO instruments: the Invalidity, Old-Age and Survivors' Benefits Convention, 1967 (No. 128), and its companion Recommendation No. 131.[17] Every State which ratifies the Convention must accept at least one of the three contingencies as an obligation.

Some of the flexibility found in other social security instruments is present in Convention No. 128: for example, temporary lower levels of coverage of the population for developing countries, and the possibility of excluding casual workers or public servants who are as well or better provided for.

Basic requirements

Invalidity is defined as the inability — likely to be permanent, or persistent after a period of temporary or initial incapacity — to engage in any gainful activity.

When a breadwinner dies, survivors' benefits must be paid at least for the widow and children.

The age for entitlement to an old-age pension is set in Convention No. 128 as "not more than 65 years or such higher age as may be fixed by the competent authority...". On the other hand, the pensionable age should, in the terms of Recommendation No. 131, be lowered if justifiable on social grounds; even if the pensionable age has not been reached, there should still be benefits — particularly for people who are unfit for work or who have been unemployed for a certain period of time.

The Older Workers Recommendation, 1980 (No. 162), [32] goes further. It calls for a flexible qualifying age for an old-age pension. The ILO's Committee of Experts on the Application of Conventions and Recommendations, in a survey of old-age benefits, [57] has come to the conclusion that it is particularly desirable to allow employees, according to health or personal preference, a degree of choice as to when they wish to start drawing their old-age pension.

The number of countries where flexible arrangements, such as voluntary early retirement, deferred retirement or progressive retirement have been introduced, is growing.

Payments

All three types of pension must be in the form of periodic cash payments, based on the total of family allowances and previous earnings or, where a flat-rate system applies, on the wage of an ordinary adult male labourer. The minimum payments are 50 per cent in cases of invalidity, and 45 per cent for old-age pensions or on the death of a breadwinner.

A 10 per cent increase on these figures is proposed in Recommendation No. 131, which nevertheless suggests a reduced benefit should be paid in cases of partial invalidity.

The Recommendation also proposes that old-age benefit should be raised if a person defers retirement after reaching the pensionable age and fulfilling the qualifying conditions. This type of arrangement is proposed in the 1966 Recommendation concerning the Status of Teachers in situations where a shortage of teachers has to be overcome.

A special consideration for teachers is introduced in the 1966 Recommendation, where it proposes that hardship allowances and cost-of-living allowances be included in the earnings to be taken into account for pension purposes.

Qualifying periods

Full invalidity or survivors' benefits require, in the terms of the Convention, a qualifying period of up to 15 years' contributions or ten years' residence, while for the old-age benefit, a period of not more than 30 years of contribution or employment or 20 years of residence are specified.

Rehabilitation and transfer of rights

States which ratify Convention No. 128 are required to provide rehabilitation services to prepare disabled persons for a resumption of their previous activities — or if this is not possible, for suitable alternative work. This is also a feature of the 1966 Recommendation.

The Convention also confirms the 1966 Recommendation proposal that teachers should be able to transfer their pension credits when moving from the employment of one authority to another.

Trend to unification of protection

In most countries, public employees were the first to benefit from social security protection, reflecting the nature of public service work and its constraints. There is now a trend, noted in 1988 by the ILO's Joint Committee on the Public Service,[54] towards unification of protection for all working people — even for all residents of a country. This trend to unification is not world wide, so it has not affected public (employees' schemes including those covering teachers everywhere.)

The Committee suggested that substantial changes, particularly resulting from the integration of public employees into a general scheme, should guarantee the rights acquired before the reform. Where there are separate schemes for established public employees and workers in the private sector, the maintenance of pension rights should be guaranteed for workers who transfer from one scheme to another. This might happen when a non-established public employee is granted a position with tenure, on a change in status of the enterprise or service — for example, through privatisation or nationalisation — or as the result of a change of job.

Conclusion

7

The adoption in 1966 of an international Recommendation concerning the Status of Teachers marked a significant step forward in efforts to recognise the important role that teachers play in education and in society as a whole. The Recommendation for the first time set out, in clear terms, a range of common standards and measures governing both the professional concerns and employment aspects of the world's educational workforce.

The 1966 Recommendation does not exist in a vacuum, however, since its provisions are reinforced by the extensive network of international labour standards adopted over the years by the International Labour Conference, and monitored by its highly developed supervisory machinery, which is designed to

ensure that governments honour the commitments they make. The standards include Conventions, which are legally binding instruments once ratified by a government, as well as Recommendations, which are used as policy guide-lines to improve social policy.

Many of these standards, whether adopted before or after the 1966 Recommendation itself came into being, are applicable to teachers. Some are relevant to teachers' employment and careers, seeking to protect security of tenure or providing a means to eliminate discrimination and encourage equality of opportunity for women teachers, older workers of the disabled. A major area covered by ILO Conventions and Recommendations consists of labour relations, including the all-important questions of consultation, collective bargaining and the right to strike protected by these standards. Remuneration and working time, including holidays and leave periods, as well as occupational health and safety standards at the workplace and social security are also fundamental targets of ILO standards.

These Conventions and Recommendations thus serve as an interlocking network to complement the detailed provisions which are set out in the 1966 Recommendation concerning the Status of Teachers. Taken together, these standards, one targeted specifically at improvements in the status of teachers, and the others which establish a more general framework for protecting workers generally, constitute an invaluable set of references for governments, private educational employers and teachers' organisations to follow in their efforts to improve the status of teachers — synonymous with upgrading education in an increasingly sophisticated world.

Annex I. Numbered list of international labour standards and of publications referred to in the text

The international standards and publications listed below are those which most directly interest, or have at least some meaning, for teachers. Reference numbers throughout the text of this publication correspond to the listing, and indicate to the reader that fuller information may be obtained by consulting the Convention, Recommendation or other document concerned.

In the case of Conventions, the number of ratifications as at 1 January 1990 is also given below.

A. International labour standards

ILO/Unesco

1. Recommendation concerning the Status of Teachers, 1966.

ILO

2. Maternity Protection Convention, 1919 (No. 3 — 28 ratifications).
   Maternity Protection Convention (Revised), 1952 (No. 103 — 26 ratifications).

3. Freedom of Association and Protection of the Right to Organise Convention, 1948 (No. 87 — 99 ratifications).

4. Employment Service Convention, 1948 (No. 88 — 71 ratifications), and Recommendation, 1948 (No. 83).

5. Protection of Wages Convention, 1949 (No. 95 — 87 ratifications), and Recommendation, 1949 (No. 85).

6. Right to Organise and Collective Bargaining Convention, 1949 (No. 98 — 115 ratifications).

7. Equal Remuneration Convention, 1951 (No. 100 — 111 ratifications), and Recommendation, 1951 (No. 90).

8. Social Security (Minimum Standards) Convention, 1952 (No. 102 — 32 ratifications).

9. Welfare Facilities Recommendation, 1956 (No. 102).

10. Discrimination (Employment and Occupation) Convention, 1958 (No. 111 — 111 ratifications), and Recommendation, 1958 (No. 111).

11. Consultation (Industrial and National Levels) Recommendation, 1960 (No. 113).

12. Workers' Housing Recommendation, 1961 (No. 115).

13. Reduction of Hours of Work Recommendation, 1962 (No. 116).

14. Guarding of Machinery Convention, 1963 (No. 119 — 39 ratifications), and Recommendation (No. 118); Maximum Weight Convention, 1967 (No. 127 — 23 ratifications), and Recommendation, 1963 (No. 118).

15. Employment Injury Benefits Convention, 1964 (No. 121 — 18 ratifications), and Recommendation, 1964 (No. 121).

16. Employment Policy Convention, 1964 (No. 122 — 73 ratifications), and Recommendation, 1964 (No. 122).

    Employment Policy (Supplementary Provisions) Recommendation, 1984 (No. 169).

17. Invalidity, Old-age and Survivors' Benefits Convention, 1967 (No. 128 — 14 ratifications), and Recommendation, 1967 (No. 131).

18. Communications within the Undertaking Recommendation, 1967 (No. 129).

19. Examination of Grievances Recommendation, 1967 (No. 130).

20. Medical Care and Sickness Benefits Convention, 1969 (No. 130 — 13 ratifications), and Recommendation, 1969 (No. 134).

21. Minimum Wage Fixing Convention, 1970 (No. 131 — 34 ratifications), and Recommendation, 1970 (No. 135).

22. Holidays with Pay Convention (Revised), 1970 (No. 132 — 19 ratifications).

23. Workers' Representatives Convention, 1971 (No. 135 — 44 ratifications), and Recommendation, 1971 (No. 143).

24. Benzene Convention, 1971 (No. 136 — 26 ratifications), and Recommendation, 1971 (No. 144).

25. Occupational Cancer Convention, 1974 (No. 139 — 22 ratifications), and Recommendation, 1974 (No. 147).

26. Paid Educational Leave Convention, 1974 (No. 140 — 22 ratifications), and Recommendation, 1974 (No. 148).

27. Human Resources Development Convention, 1975 (No. 142 — 45 ratifications), and Recommendation, 1975 (No. 150).

28. Tripartite Consultation (International Labour Standards) Convention, 1976 (No. 144 — 47 ratifications), and Tripartite Consultation (Activities of the International Labour Organisation) Recommendation, 1976 (No. 152).

29. Working Environment (Air Pollution, Noise and Vibration) Convention, 1977 (No. 148 — 24 ratifications), and Recommendation, 1977 (No. 156).

30. Labour Administration Convention, 1978 (No. 150 – 34 ratifications), and Recommendation, 1978 (No. 158).
31. Labour Relations (Public Service) Convention, 1978 (No. 151 – 22 ratifications), and Recommendation, 1978 (No. 159).
32. Older Workers Recommendation, 1980 (No. 162).
33. Collective Bargaining Convention, 1981 (No. 154 – 11 ratifications), and Recommendation, 1981 (No. 163).
34. Occupational Safety and Health Convention, 1981 (No. 155 – 12 ratifications), and Recommendation, 1981 (No. 164).
35. Workers with Family Responsibilities Convention, 1981 (No. 156 – 16 ratifications), and Recommendation, 1981 (No. 165).
36. Termination of Employment Convention, 1982 (No. 158 – 12 ratifications), and Recommendation, 1982 (No. 166).
37. Vocational Rehabilitation (Disabled) Recommendation, 1955 (No. 99).
    Vocational Rehabilitation and Employment (Disabled Persons) Convention, 1983 (No. 159 – 30 ratifications), and Recommendation, 1983 (No. 168).
38. Labour Statistics Convention, 1985 (No. 160 – 15 ratifications), and Recommendation, 1985 (No. 170).
39. Occupational Health Services Convention, 1985 (No. 161 – 9 ratifications), and Recommendation, 1985 (No. 171).
40. Asbestos Convention, 1986 (No. 162 – 6 ratifications), and Recommendation, 1986 (No. 172).
41. Employment Promotion and Protection against Unemployment Convention, 1988 (No. 168 – not yet in force), and Recommendation, 1988 (No. 176).

B. Publications

42. *Teachers' pay*, Geneva, ILO, 1978.
43. *Social security for teachers*, Geneva, ILO, 1979.
44. *Report of the Committee of Experts on the Application of Conventions and Recommendations*, Report III (Part 4A), International Labour Conference, 65th Session, Geneva, 1979.
45. *Report of the Joint Meeting on Conditions of Work of Teachers,* Geneva, ILO, 1981.
46. *Freedom of association and collective bargaining: General survey by the Committee of Experts on the Application of Conventions and Recommendations*, Report III (Part 4B), International Labour Conference, 69th Session, Geneva, 1983.
47. *Report of the Committee of Experts on the Application of Conventions and Recommendations*, Report III (Part 4A), International Labour Conference, 70th Session, Geneva, 1984.

48. *Working Time; Reduction of Hours of Work, Weekly Rest and Holidays with Pay: General Survey by the Committee of Experts on the Application of Conventions and Recommendations*, Report III (Part 4B), International Labour Conference, 70th Session, Geneva, 1984.

49. *Introduction to social security*, 3rd ed., Geneva, ILO, 1984.

50. *The status of teachers*. Joint commentaries by the ILO and Unesco on the Recommendation concerning the Status of Teachers, 1966, Geneva, ILO, 1984.

51. *Freedom of Association: Digest of Decisions and Principles of the Freedom of Association Committee*, 3rd ed., Geneva, ILO, 1985.

52. Surveys on the possible updating of the Recommendation concerning the Status of Teachers and on the Usefulness of the Instrument. Paris, ILO/Unesco, 1986.

53. *Equal Remuneration: General Survey by the Committee of Experts on the Application of Conventions and Recommendations*, Report III (Part 4B). 72nd Session of the International Labour Conference, Geneva, 1986.

54. Joint Committee on the Public Service, Fourth Session, Geneva, 1988. *General report* (Part I).

55. *Joint ILO/Unesco Committee of Experts on the Application of the Recommendation concerning the Status of Teachers*. Report of Fifth Session, Geneva, ILO/Unesco, 1988.

56. *Equity in Employment and Occupation: General Survey by the Committee of Experts on the Application of Conventions and Recommendations*, Report III (Part. 4B). 75th Session of the International Labour Conference, Geneva, 1988.

57. *Social Security Protection in Old Age: General Survey of the Committee of Experts on the Application of Conventions and Recommendations*. Report III (Part 4B). 76th Session of the International Labour Conference, Geneva, 1989.

58. Joint Committee on the Public Service, Fourth Session, Geneva, 1988. Report III: *Social security, including social protection of public employees in respect of invalidity, retirement and survivors' benefits*.

Annex II. Recommendation concerning the Status of Teachers

Adopted by the Special Intergovernmental Conference on the Status of Teachers, Paris, 5 October 1966

The Special Intergovernmental Conference on the Status of Teachers,

Recalling that the right to education is a fundamental human right,

Conscious of the responsibility of the States for the provision of proper education for all in fulfilment of Article 26 of the Universal Declaration of Human Rights, of Principles 5, 7 and 10 of the Declaration of the Rights of the Child and of the United Nations Declaration concerning the Promotion among Youth of the Ideals of Peace, Mutual Respect and Understanding between Peoples,

Aware of the need for more extensive and widespread general and technical and vocational education, with a view to making full use of all the talent and intelligence available as an essential contribution to continued moral and cultural progress and economic and social advancement,

Recognising the essential role of teachers in educational advancement and the importance of their contribution to the development of man and modern society,

Concerned to ensure that teachers enjoy the status commensurate with this role,

Taking into account the great diversity of the laws, regulations and customs which, in different countries, determine the patterns and organisation of education,

Taking also into account the diversity of the arrangements which in different countries apply to teaching staff, in particular according to whether the regulations concerning the public service apply to them,

Convinced that in spite of these differences similar questions arise in all countries with regard to the status of teachers and that these questions call for the application of a set of common standards and measures, which it is the purpose of this Recommendation to set out,

Noting the terms of existing international conventions which are applicable to teachers, and in particular of instruments concerned with basic human rights such as the Freedom of Association and Protection of the Right to Organise Convention, 1948, the Right to Organise and Collective Bargaining Convention, 1949, the Equal Remuneration Convention, 1951, and the Discrimination (Employment and Occupation) Convention, 1958, adopted by the General Conference of the International Labour Organisation, and the Convention against Discrimination in Education, 1960, adopted by the General Conference of the United Nations Educational, Scientific and Cultural Organisation,

Noting also the recommendations on various aspects of the preparation and the status of teachers in primary and secondary schools adopted by the International Conference on Public Education convened jointly by the United Nations Educational, Scientific and Cultural Organisation and the International Bureau of Education, and the Recommendation concerning Technical and Vocational Education, 1962, adopted by the General Conference of the United Nations Educational, Scientific and Cultural Organisation,

Desiring to supplement existing standards by provisions relating to problems of peculiar concern to teachers and to remedy the problems of teacher shortage;

Has adopted this Recommendation:

I. Definitions

1. For the purpose of the Recommendation:

(a) the word "teacher" covers all those persons in schools who are responsible for the education of pupils;

(b) the expression "status" as used in relation to teachers means both the standing or regard accorded them, as evidenced by the level of appreciation of the importance of their function and of their competence in performing it, and the working conditions, remuneration and other material benefits accorded them relative to other professional groups.

II. Scope

2. This Recommendation applies to all teachers in both public and private schools up to the completion of the secondary stage of education whether nursery, kindergarten, primary, intermediate or secondary, including those providing technical, vocational, or art education.

III. Guiding principles

3. Education from the earliest school years should be directed to the all-round development of the human personality and to the spiritual, moral, social, cultural and economic progress of the community, as well as to the inculcation of deep respect for human rights and fundamental freedoms; within the framework of these values the utmost importance should be attached to the contribution to be made by education to peace and to understanding, tolerance and friendship among all nations and among racial or religious groups.

4. It should be recognised that advance in education depends largely on the qualifications and ability of the teaching staff in general and on the human, pedagogical and technical qualities of the individual teachers.

5. The status of teachers should be commensurate with the needs of education as assessed in the light of educational aims and objectives; it should be recognised that the proper status of teachers and due public regard for the profession of teaching are of major importance for the full realisation of these aims and objectives.

6. Teaching should be regarded as a profession: it is a form of public service which requires of teachers expert knowledge and specialised skills, acquired and maintained through rigorous and continuing study; it calls also for a sense of personal and corporate responsibility for the education and welfare of the pupils in their charge.

7. All aspects of the preparation and employment of teachers should be free from any form of discrimination on grounds of race, colour, sex, religion, political opinion, national or social origin, or economic condition.

8. Working conditions for teachers should be such as will best promote effective learning and enable teachers to concentrate on their professional tasks.

9. Teachers' organisations should be recognised as a force which can contribute greatly to educational advance and which therefore should be associated with the determination of educational policy.

IV. Educational objectives and policies

10. Appropriate measures should be taken in each country to the extent necessary to formulate comprehensive educational policies consistent with the Guiding Principles, drawing on all available resources, human and otherwise. In so doing, the competent authorities should take account of the consequences for teachers of the following principles and objectives:

(a) it is the fundamental right of every child to be provided with the fullest possible educational opportunities; due attention should be paid to children requiring special educational treatment;

(b) all facilities should be made available equally to enable every person to enjoy his right to education without discrimination on grounds of sex, race, colour, religion, political opinion, national or social origin, or economic condition;

(c) since education is a service of fundamental importance in the general public interest, it should be recognised as a responsibility of the State, which should provide an adequate network of schools, free education in these schools and material assistance to needy pupils; this should not be construed so as to interfere with the liberty of the parents and, when applicable, legal guardians to choose for their children schools other than those established by the State, or so as to interfere with the liberty of individuals and bodies to establish and direct educational institutions which conform to such minimum educational standards as may be laid down or approved by the State;

(d) since education is an essential factor in economic growth, educational planning should form an integral part of total economic and social planning undertaken to improve living conditions;

(e) since education is a continuous process, the various branches of the teaching service should be so co-ordinated as both to improve the quality of education for all pupils and to enhance the status of teachers;

(f) there should be free access to a flexible system of schools, properly interrelated, so that nothing restricts the opportunities for each child to progress to any level in any type of education;

(g) as an educational objective, no State should be satisfied with mere quantity, but should seek also to improve quality;

(h) in education both long-term and short-term planning and programming are necessary; the efficient integration in the community of today's pupils will depend more on future needs than on present requirements;

(i) all educational planning should include at each stage early provision for the training, and the further training, of sufficient numbers of fully competent and qualified teachers of the country concerned who are familiar with the life of their people and able to teach in the mother tongue;

(j) co-ordinated systematic and continuing research and action in the field of teacher preparation and in-service training are essential, including, at the international level, co-operative projects and the exchange of research findings;

(k) there should be close co-operation between the competent authorities, organisations of teachers, of employers and workers, and of parents as well as cultural organisations and institutions of learning and research, for the purpose of defining educational policy and its precise objectives;

(l) as the achievement of the aims and objectives of education largely depends on the financial means made available to it, high priority should be given, in all countries, to setting aside, within the national budgets, an adequate proportion of the national income for the development of education.

V. Preparation for the profession

Selection

11. Policy governing entry into preparation for teaching should rest on the need to provide society with an adequate supply of teachers who possess the necessary moral, intellectual and physical qualities and who have the required professional knowledge and skills.

12. To meet this need, educational authorities should provide adequate inducements to prepare for teaching and sufficient places in appropriate institutions.

13. Completion of an approved course in an appropriate teacher-preparation institution should be required of all persons entering the profession.

14. Admission to teacher preparation should be based on the completion of appropriate secondary education, and the evidence of the possession of personal qualities likely to help the persons concerned to become worthy members of the profession.

15. While the general standards for admission to teacher preparation should be maintained, persons who may lack some of the formal academic requirements for admission, but who possess valuable experience, particularly in technical and vocational fields, may be admitted.

16. Adequate grants or financial assistance should be available to students preparing for teaching to enable them to follow the courses provided and to live decently; as far as possible, the competent authorities should seek to establish a system of free teacher-preparation institutions.

17. Information concerning the opportunities and the grants or financial assistance for teacher preparation should be readily available to students and other persons who may wish to prepare for teaching.

18. (1) Fair consideration should be given to the value of teacher-preparation programmes completed in other countries as establishing in whole or in part the right to practise teaching.

(2) Steps should be taken with a view to achieving international recognition of teaching credentials conferring professional status in terms of standards agreed to internationally.

Teacher-preparation programmes

19. The purpose of a teacher-preparation programme should be to develop in each student his general education and personal culture, his ability to teach and educate others, an awareness of the principles which underlie good human relations, within and across national boundaries, and a sense of responsibility to contribute both by teaching and by example to social, cultural, and economic progress.

20. Fundamentally, a teacher-preparation programme should include:

(a) general studies;

(b) study of the main elements of philosophy, psychology, sociology as applied to education, the theory and history of education, and of comparative education, experimental pedagogy, school administration and methods of teaching the various subjects;

(c) studies related to the student's intended field of teaching;

(d) practice in teaching and in conducting extra-curricular activities under the guidance of fully qualified teachers.

21. (1) All teachers should be prepared in general, special and pedagogical subjects in universities, or in institutions on a level comparable to universities, or else in special institutions for the preparation of teachers.

(2) The content of teacher-preparation programmes may reasonably vary according to the tasks the teachers are required to perform in different types of schools, such

as establishments for handicapped children or technical and vocational schools. In the latter case, the programmes might include some practical experience to be acquired in industry, commerce or agriculture.

22. A teacher-preparation programme may provide for a professional course either concurrently with or subsequent to a course of personal academic or specialised education or skill cultivation.

23. Education for teaching should normally be full time; special arrangements may be made for older entrants to the profession and persons in other exceptional categories to undertake all or part of their course on a part-time basis, on condition that the content of such courses and the standards of attainment are on the same level as those of the full-time courses.

24. Consideration should be given to the desirability of providing for the education of different types of teachers, whether primary, secondary, technical, specialist or vocational teachers, in institutions organically related or geographically adjacent to one another.

Teacher-preparation institutions

25. The staff of teacher-preparation institutions should be qualified to teach in their own discipline at a level equivalent to that of higher education. The staff teaching pedagogical subjects should have had experience of teaching in schools and wherever possible should have this experience periodically refreshed by secondment to teaching duties in schools.

26. Research and experimentation in education and in the teaching of particular subjects should be promoted through the provision of research facilities in teacher-preparation institutions and research work by their staff and students. All staff concerned with teacher education should be aware of the findings of research in the field with which they are concerned and endeavour to pass on its results to students.

27. Students as well as staff should have the opportunity of expressing their views on the arrangements governing the life, work and discipline of a teacher-preparation institution.

28. Teacher-preparation institutions should form a focus of development in the education service, both keeping schools abreast of the results of research and methodological progress, and reflecting in their own work the experience of schools and teachers.

29. The teacher-preparation institutions should, either severally or jointly, and in collaboration with another institution of higher education or with the competent education authorities, or not, be responsible for certifying that the student has satisfactorily completed the course.

30. School authorities, in co-operation with teacher-preparation institutions, should take appropriate measures to provide the newly trained teachers with an employment in keeping with their preparation, and individual wishes and circumstances.

VI. Further education for teachers

31. Authorities and teachers should recognise the importance of in-service education designed to secure a systematic improvement of the quality and content of education and of teaching techniques.

32. Authorities, in consultation with teachers' organisations, should promote the establishment of a wide system of in-service education, available free to all teachers. Such a system should provide a variety of arrangements and should involve the participation of teacher-preparation institutions, scientific and cultural institutions, and teachers' organisations. Refresher courses should be provided, especially for teachers returning to teaching after a break in service.

33. (1) Courses and other appropriate facilities should be so designed as to enable teachers to improve their qualifications, to alter or enlarge the scope of their work or seek promotion and to keep up to date with their subject and field of education as regards both content and method.

(2) Measures should be taken to make books and other material available to teachers to improve their general education and professional qualifications.

34. Teachers should be given both the opportunities and the incentives to participate in courses and facilities and should take full advantage of them.

35. School authorities should make every endeavour to ensure that schools can apply relevant research findings both in the subjects of study and in teaching methods.

36. Authorities should encourage and, as far as possible, assist teachers to travel in their own country and abroad, either in groups or individually, with a view to their further education.

37. It would be desirable that measures taken for the preparation and further education of teachers should be developed and supplemented by financial and technical co-operation on an international or regional basis.

VII. Employment and career

Entry into the teaching profession

38. In collaboration with teachers' organisations, policy governing recruitment into employment should be clearly defined at the appropriate level and rules should be established laying down the teachers' obligations and rights.

39. A probationary period on entry to teaching should be recognised both by teachers and by employers as the opportunity for the encouragement and helpful initiation of the entrant and for the establishment and maintenance of proper professional standards as well as the teacher's own development of his practical teaching proficiency. The normal duration of probation should be known in advance and the conditions for its satisfactory completion should be strictly related to professional competence. If the teacher is failing to complete his probation satisfactorily, he should be informed of the reasons and should have the right to make representations.

Advancement and promotion

40. Teachers should be able, subject to their having the necessary qualifications, to move from one type or level of school to another within the education service.

41. The organisation and structure of an education service, including that of individual schools, should provide adequate opportunities for and recognition of additional responsibilities to be exercised by individual teachers, on condition that those responsibilities are not detrimental to the quality or regularity of their teaching work.

42. Consideration should be given to the advantages of schools sufficiently large for pupils to have the benefits and staff the opportunities to be derived from a range of responsibilities being carried by different teachers.

43. Posts of responsibility in education, such as that of inspector, educational administrator, director of education or other posts of special responsibility, should be given as far as possible to experienced teachers.

44. Promotion should be based on an objective assessment of the teacher's qualifications for the new post, by reference to strictly professional criteria laid down in consultation with teachers' organisations.

Security of tenure

45. Stability of employment and security of tenure in the profession are essential in the interests of education as well as in that of the teacher and should be safeguarded even when changes in the organisation of or within a school system are made.

46. Teachers should be adequately protected against arbitrary action affecting their professional standing or career.

Disciplinary procedures related to breaches of professional conduct

47. Disciplinary measures applicable to teachers guilty of breaches of professional conduct should be clearly defined. The proceedings and any resulting action should only be made public if the teacher so requests, except where prohibition from teaching is involved or the protection or well-being of the pupils so requires.

48. The authorities or bodies competent to propose or apply sanctions and penalties should be clearly designated.

49. Teachers' organisations should be consulted when the machinery to deal with disciplinary matters is established.

50. Every teacher should enjoy equitable safeguards at each stage of any disciplinary procedure, and in particular:

(a) the right to be informed in writing of the allegations and the grounds for them;

(b) the right to full access to the evidence in the case;

(c) the right to defend himself and to be defended by a representative of his choice, adequate time being given to the teacher for the preparation of his defence;

(d) the right to be informed in writing of the decisions reached and the reasons for them;

(e) the right to appeal to clearly designated competent authorities or bodies.

51. Authorities should recognise that effectiveness of disciplinary safeguards as well as discipline itself would be greatly enhanced if the teachers were judged with the participation of their peers.

52. The provisions of the foregoing paragraphs 47-51 do not in any way affect the procedures normally applicable under national laws or regulations to acts punishable under criminal laws.

Medical examinations

53. Teachers should be required to undergo periodical medical examinations, which should be provided free.

Women teachers with family responsibilities

54. Marriage should not be considered a bar to the appointment or to the continued employment of women teachers, nor should it affect remuneration or other conditions of work.

55. Employers should be prohibited from terminating contracts of service for reasons of pregnancy and maternity leave.

56. Arrangements such as crèches or nurseries should be considered where desirable to take care of the children of teachers with family responsibilities.

57. Measures should be taken to permit women teachers with family responsibilities to obtain teaching posts in the locality of their homes and to enable married couples, both of whom are teachers, to teach in the same general neighbourhood or in one and the same school.

58. In appropriate circumstances women teachers with family responsibilities who have left the profession before retirement age should be encouraged to return to teaching.

Part-time service

59. Authorities and schools should recognise the value of part-time service given, in case of need, by qualified teachers who for some reason cannot give full-time service.

60. Teachers employed regularly on a part-time basis should:

(a) receive proportionately the same remuneration and enjoy the same basic conditions of employment as teachers employed on a full-time basis;

(b) be granted rights corresponding to those of teachers employed on a full-time basis as regards holidays with pay, sick leave and maternity leave, subject to the same eligibility requirements; and

(c) be entitled to adequate and appropriate social security protection, including coverage under employers' pension schemes.

VIII.   The rights and responsibilities of teachers

Professional freedom

61. The teaching profession should enjoy academic freedom in the discharge of professional duties. Since teachers are particularly qualified to judge the teaching aids and methods most suitable for their pupils, they should be given the essential role in the choice and the adaptation of teaching material, the selection of textbooks and the application of teaching methods, within the framework of approved programmes, and with the assistance of the educational authorities.

62. Teachers and their organisations should participate in the development of new courses, textbooks and teaching aids.

63. Any systems of inspection or supervision should be designed to encourage and help teachers in the performance of their professional tasks and should be such as not to diminish the freedom, initiative and responsibility of teachers.

64. (1) Where any kind of direct assessment of the teacher's work is required, such assessment should be objective and should be made known to the teacher.

(2) Teachers should have a right to appeal against assessments which they deem to be unjustified.

65. Teachers should be free to make use of such evaluation techniques as they may deem useful for the appraisal of pupils' progress, but should ensure that no unfairness to individual pupils results.

66. The authorities should give due weight to the recommendations of teachers regarding the suitability of individual pupils for courses and further education of different kinds.

67. Every possible effort should be made to promote close co-operation between teachers and parents in the interests of pupils, but teachers should be protected against unfair or unwarranted interference by parents in matters which are essentially the teacher's professional responsibility.

68. (1) Parents having a complaint against a school or a teacher should be given the opportunity of discussing it in the first instance with the school principal and the teacher concerned. Any complaint subsequently addressed to higher authority should be put in writing and a copy should be supplied to the teacher.

(2) Investigations of complaints should be so conducted that the teachers are given a fair opportunity to defend themselves and that no publicity is given to the proceedings.

69. While teachers should exercise the utmost care to avoid accidents to pupils, employers of teachers should safeguard them against the risk of having damages assessed against them in the event of injury to pupils occurring at school or in school activities away from the school premises or grounds.

Responsibilities of teachers

70. Recognising that the status of their profession depends to a considerable extent upon teachers themselves, all teachers should seek to achieve the highest possible standards in all their professional work.

71. Professional standards relating to teacher performance should be defined and maintained with the participation of the teachers' organisations.

72. Teachers and teachers' organisations should seek to co-operate fully with authorities in the interests of the pupils, of the education service and of society generally.

73. Codes of ethics or of conduct should be established by the teachers' organisations, since such codes greatly contribute to ensuring the prestige of the profession and the exercise of professional duties in accordance with agreed principles.

74. Teachers should be prepared to take their part in extra-curricular activities for the benefit of pupils and adults.

Relations between teachers and the education service as a whole

75. In order that teachers may discharge their responsibilities, authorities should establish and regularly use recognised means of consultation with teachers' organisations on such matters as educational policy, school organisation, and new developments in the education service.

76. Authorities and teachers should recognise the importance of the participation of teachers, through their organisations and in other ways, in steps designed to improve the quality of the education service, in educational research, and in the development and dissemination of new improved methods.

77. Authorities should facilitate the establishment and the work of panels designed, within a school or within a broader framework, to promote the co-operation of teachers of the same subject and should take due account of the opinions and suggestions of such panels.

78. Administrative and other staff who are responsible for aspects of the education service should seek to establish good relations with teachers and this approach should be equally reciprocated.

Rights of teachers

79. The participation of teachers in social and public life should be encouraged in the interests of the teacher's personal development, of the education service and of society as a whole.

80. Teachers should be free to exercise all civic rights generally enjoyed by citizens and should be eligible for public office.

81. Where the requirements of public office are such that the teacher has to relinquish his teaching duties, he should be retained in the profession for seniority and pension purposes and should be able to return to his previous post or to an equivalent post after his term of public office has expired.

82. Both salaries and working conditions for teachers should be determined through the process of negotiation between teachers' organisations and the employers of teachers.

83. Statutory or voluntary machinery should be established whereby the right of teachers to negotiate through their organisations with their employers, either public or private, is assured.

84. Appropriate joint machinery should be set up to deal with the settlement of disputes between the teachers and their employers arising out of terms and conditions of employment. If the means and procedures established for these purposes should be exhausted or if there should be a breakdown in negotiations between the parties, teachers' organisations should have the right to take such other steps as are normally open to other organisations in the defence of their legitimate interests.

IX. Conditions for effective teaching and learning

85. Since the teacher is a valuable specialist, his work should be so organised and assisted as to avoid waste of his time and energy.

Class size

86. Class size should be such as to permit the teacher to give the pupils individual attention. From time to time provision may be made for small group or even individual instruction for such purposes as remedial work, and on occasion for large group instruction employing audio-visual aids.

Ancillary staff

87. With a view to enabling teachers to concentrate on their professional tasks, schools should be provided with ancillary staff to perform non-teaching duties.

Teaching aids

88. (1) Authorities should provide teachers and pupils with modern aids to teaching. Such aids should not be regarded as a substitute for the teacher but as a means of improving the quality of teaching and extending to a larger number of pupils the benefits of education.

(2) Authorities should promote research into the use of such aids and encourage teachers to participate actively in such research.

Hours of work

89. The hours teachers are required to work per day and per week should be established in consultation with teachers' organisations.

90. In fixing hours of teaching, account should be taken of all factors which are relevant to the teacher's work load, such as:

(a) the number of pupils with whom the teacher is required to work per day and per week;

(b) the necessity to provide time for adequate planning and preparation of lessons and for evaluation of work;

(c) the number of different lessons assigned to be taught each day;

(d) the demands upon the time of the teacher imposed by participation in research, in co-curricular and extra-curricular activities, in supervisory duties and in counselling of pupils;

(e) the desirability of providing time in which teachers may report to and consult with parents regarding pupil progress.

91. Teachers should be provided time necessary for taking part in in-service training programmes.

92. Participation of teachers in extra-curricular activities should not constitute an excessive burden and should not interfere with the fulfilment of the main duties of the teacher.

93. Teachers assigned special educational responsibilities in addition to classroom instruction should have their normal hours of teaching reduced correspondingly.

Annual holidays with pay

94. All teachers should enjoy a right to adequate annual vacation with full pay.

Study leave

95. (1) Teachers should be granted study leave on full or partial pay at intervals.

(2) The period of study leave should be counted for seniority and pension purposes.

(3) Teachers in areas which are remote from population centres and are recognised as such by the public authorities should be given study leave more frequently.

Special leave

96. Leave of absence granted within the framework of bilateral and multilateral cultural exchanges should be considered as service.

97. Teachers attached to technical assistance projects should be granted leave of absence and their seniority, eligibility for promotion and pension rights in the home country should be safeguarded. In addition special arrangements should be made to cover their extraordinary expenses.

98. Foreign guest teachers should similarly be given leave of absence by their home countries and have their seniority and pension rights safeguarded.

99. (1) Teachers should be granted occasional leave of absence with full pay to enable them to participate in the activities of their organisations.

(2) Teachers should have the right to take up office in their organisations; in such case their entitlements should be similar to those of teachers holding public office.

100. Teachers should be granted leave of absence with full pay for adequate personal reasons under arrangements specified in advance of employment.

Sick leave and maternity leave

101. (1) Teachers should be entitled to sick leave with pay.

(2) In determining the period during which full or partial pay shall be payable, account should be taken of cases in which it is necessary for teachers to be isolated from pupils for long periods.

102. Effect should be given to the standards laid down by the International Labour Organisation in the field of maternity protection, and in particular the Maternity Protection Convention, 1919, and the Maternity Protection Convention (Revised), 1952, as well as to the standards referred to in paragraph 126 of this Recommendation.

103. Women teachers with children should be encouraged to remain in the service by such measures as enabling them, at their request, to take additional unpaid leave of up to one year after childbirth without loss of employment, all rights resulting from employment being fully safeguarded.

Teacher exchange

104. Authorities should recognise the value both to the education service and to teachers themselves of professional and cultural exchanges between countries and of travel abroad on the part of teachers; they should seek to extend such opportunities and take account of the experience acquired abroad by individual teachers.

105. Recruitment for such exchanges should be arranged without any discrimination, and the persons concerned should not be considered as representing any particular political view.

106. Teachers who travel in order to study and work abroad should be given adequate facilities to do so and proper safeguards of their posts and status.

107. Teachers should be encouraged to share teaching experience gained abroad with other members of the profession.

School buildings

108. School buildings should be safe and attractive in overall design and functional in layout; they should lend themselves to effective teaching, and to use for extra-curricular activities and, especially in rural areas, as a community centre; they should be constructed in accordance with established sanitary standards and with a view to durability, adaptability and easy, economic maintenance.

109. Authorities should ensure that school premises are properly maintained, so as not to threaten in any way the health and safety of pupils and teachers.

110. In the planning of new schools, representative teacher opinion should be consulted. In providing new or additional accommodation for an existing school the staff of the school concerned should be consulted.

Special provisions for teachers in rural or remote areas

111. (1) Decent housing, preferably free or at a subsidised rental, should be provided for teachers and their families in areas remote from population centres and recognised as such by the public authorities.

(2) In countries where teachers, in addition to their normal teaching duties, are expected to promote and stimulate community activities, development plans and programmes should include provision for appropriate accommodation for teachers.

112. (1) On appointment or transfer to schools in remote areas, teachers should be paid removal and travel expenses for themselves and their families.

(2) Teachers in such areas should, where necessary, be given special travel facilities to enable them to maintain their professional standards.

(3) Teachers transferred to remote areas should, as an inducement, be reimbursed their travel expenses from their place of work to their home town once a year when they go on leave.

113. Whenever teachers are exposed to particular hardships, they should be compensated by the payment of special hardship allowances which should be included in earnings taken into account for pension purposes.

X. Teachers' salaries

114. Amongst the various factors which affect the status of teachers, particular importance should be attached to salary, seeing that in present world conditions other factors, such as the standing or regard accorded them and the level of appreciation of

the importance of their function, are largely dependent, as in other comparable professions, on the economic position in which they are placed.

115. Teachers' salaries should:

(a) reflect the importance to society of the teaching function and hence the importance
of teachers as well as the responsibilities of all kinds which fall upon them from the
time of their entry into the service;

(b) compare favourably with salaries paid in other occupations requiring similar or
equivalent qualifications;

(c) provide teachers with the means to ensure a reasonable standard of living for themselves and their families as well as to invest in further education or in the pursuit
of cultural activities, thus enhancing their professional qualification;

(d) take account of the fact that certain posts require higher qualifications and
experience and carry greater responsibilities.

116. Teachers should be paid on the basis of salary scales established in agreement
with the teachers' organisations. In no circumstances should qualified teachers during
a probationary period or if employed on a temporary basis be paid on a lower salary
scale than that laid down for established teachers.

117. The salary structure should be planned so as not to give rise to injustices or
anomalies tending to lead to friction between different groups of teachers.

118. Where a maximum number of class contact hours is laid down, a teacher
whose regular schedule exceeds the normal maximum should receive additional
remuneration on an approved scale.

119. Salary differentials should be based on objective criteria such as levels of
qualification, years of experience or degrees of responsibility, but the relationship
between the lowest and the highest salary should be of a reasonable order.

120. In establishing the placement on a basic salary scale of a teacher of vocational
or technical subjects who may have no academic degree, allowance should be made for
the value of his practical training and experience.

121. Teachers' salaries should be calculated on an annual basis.

122. (1) Advancement within the grade through salary increments granted at
regular, preferably annual, intervals should be provided.

(2) The progression from the minimum to the maximum of the basic salary scale
should not extend over a period longer than ten to 15 years.

(3) Teachers should be granted salary increments for service performed during
periods of probationary or temporary appointment.

123. (1) Salary scales for teachers should be reviewed periodically to take into
account such factors as a rise in the cost of living, increased productivity leading to
higher standards of living in the country or a general upward movement in wage or
salary levels.

(2) Where a system of salary adjustments automatically following a cost-of-living
index has been adopted, the choice of index should be determined with the participation

of the teachers' organisations and any cost-of-living allowance granted should be regarded as an integral part of earnings taken into account for pension purposes.

124. No merit rating system for purposes of salary determination should be introduced or applied without prior consultation with and acceptance by the teachers' organisations concerned.

XI. Social security

General provisions

125. All teachers, regardless of the type of school in which they serve, should enjoy the same or similar social security protection. Protection should be extended to periods of probation and of training for those who are regularly employed as teachers.

126. (1) Teachers should be protected by social security measures in respect of all the contingencies included in the International Labour Organisation's Social Security (Minimum Standards) Convention, 1952, namely by medical care, sickness benefit, unemployment benefit, old-age benefit, employment injury benefit, family benefit, maternity benefit, invalidity benefit and survivors' benefit.

(2) The standards of social security provided for teachers should be at least as favourable as those set out in the relevant instruments of the International Labour Organisation and in particular the Social Security (Minimum Standards) Convention, 1952.

(3) Social security benefits for teachers should be granted as a matter of right.

127. The social security protection of teachers should take account of their particular conditions of employment, as indicated in paragraphs 128-140.

Medical care

128. In regions where there is a scarcity of medical facilities, teachers should be paid travelling expenses necessary to obtain appropriate medical care.

Sickness benefit

129. (1) Sickness benefit should be granted throughout any period of incapacity for work involving suspension of earnings.

(2) It should be paid from the first day in each case of suspension of earnings.

(3) Where the duration of sickness benefit is limited to a specified period, provisions should be made for extensions in cases in which it is necessary for teachers to be isolated from pupils.

Employment injury benefit

130. Teachers should be protected against the consequences of injuries suffered not only during teaching at school but also when engaged in school activities away from the school premises or grounds.

131. Certain infectious diseases prevalent among children should be regarded as occupational diseases when contracted by teachers who have been exposed to them by virtue of their contact with pupils.

Old-age benefit

132. Pension credits earned by a teacher under any education authority within a country should be portable should the teacher transfer to employment under any other authority within that country.

133. Taking account of national regulations, teachers who, in case of a duly recognised teacher shortage, continue in service after qualifying for a pension should either receive credit in the calculation of the pension for the additional years of service or be able to gain a supplementary pension through an appropriate agency.

134. Old-age benefit should be so related to final earnings that the teacher may continue to maintain an adequate living standard.

Invalidity benefit

135. Invalidity benefit should be payable to teachers who are forced to discontinue teaching because of physical or mental disability. Provision should be made for the granting of pensions where the contingency is not covered by extended sickness benefit or other means.

136. Where disability is only partial in that the teacher is able to teach part time, partial invalidity benefit should be payable.

137. (1) Invalidity benefit should be so related to final earnings that the teacher may continue to maintain an adequate living standard.

(2) Provision should be made for medical care and allied benefits with a view to restoring or, where this is not possible, improving the health of disabled teachers, as well as for rehabilitation services designed to prepare disabled teachers, wherever possible, for the resumption of their previous activity.

Survivors' benefit

138. The conditions of eligibility for survivors' benefit and the amount of such benefit should be such as to enable survivors to maintain an adequate standard of living and as to secure the welfare and education of surviving dependent children.

Means of providing social security for teachers

139. (1) The social security protection of teachers should be assured as far as possible through a general scheme applicable to employed persons in the public sector or in the private sector as appropriate.

(2) Where no general scheme is in existence for one or more of the contingencies to be covered, special schemes, statutory or non-statutory, should be established.

(3) Where the level of benefits under a general scheme is below that provided for in this Recommendation, it should be brought up to the recommended standard by means of supplementary schemes.

140. Consideration should be given to the possibility of associating representatives of teachers' organisations with the administration of special and supplementary schemes, including the investment of their funds.

XII. The teacher shortage

141. (1) It should be a guiding principle that any severe supply problem should be dealt with by measures which are recognised as exceptional, which do not detract from or endanger in any way professional standards already established or to be established and which minimise educational loss to pupils.

(2) Recognising that certain expedients designed to deal with the shortage of teachers, such as over-large classes and the unreasonable extension of hours of teaching duty are incompatible with the aims and objectives of education and are detrimental to the pupils, the competent authorities as a matter of urgency should take steps to render these expedients unnecessary and to discontinue them.

142. In developing countries, where supply considerations may necessitate short-term intensive emergency preparation programmes for teachers, a fully professional, extensive programme should be available in order to produce corps of professionally prepared teachers competent to guide and direct the educational enterprise.

143. (1) Students admitted to training in short-term, emergency programmes should be selected in terms of the standards applying to admission to the normal professional programme, or even higher ones, to ensure that they will be capable of subsequently completing the requirements of the full programme.

(2) Arrangements and special facilities, including extra study leave on full pay, should enable such students to complete their qualifications in service.

144. (1) As far as possible, unqualified personnel should be required to work under the close supervision and direction of professionally qualified teachers.

(2) As a condition of continued employment such persons should be required to obtain or complete their qualifications.

145. Authorities should recognise that improvements in the social and economic status of teachers, their living and working conditions, their terms of employment and their career prospects are the best means of overcoming any existing shortage of competent and experienced teachers, and of attracting to and retaining in the teaching profession substantial numbers of fully qualified persons.

XIII.   Final provision

146. Where teachers enjoy a status which is, in certain respects, more favourable than that provided for in this Recommendation, its terms should not be invoked to diminish the status already granted.

www.ingramcontent.com/pod-product-compliance
Lightning Source LLC
Chambersburg PA
CBHW031950190326
41519CB00007B/746